MW00950886

The 30-Minute
Pelz Diet
COOKBOOK

150+ Quick Menopause-Friendly Recipes Inspired by Dr. Mindy Pelz for Hormone Balance, Energy, and Weight Loss | With Fasting and Gut Health Tips for Women Over 40

28-Day Meal Plan Included

Molly Wise

Table of Contents

Introduction

About Dr. Mindy Pelz and The 10-Minute Pelz Diet

In a world where women's health needs are often overlooked or generalized, Dr. Mindy Pelz has emerged as a prominent advocate for women over 40 seeking natural, effective strategies for better health. Dr. Pelz's work shines a light on the unique hormonal challenges women face, particularly during midlife and menopause, offering practical guidance to help them navigate these changes through nutrition, lifestyle, and a few key diet principles. The "10-Minute Pelz Diet" is inspired by her philosophy that small, manageable adjustments can yield powerful results without the stress or intensity of extreme dieting, long workouts, or complicated routines.

Through her research, clinical experience, and passion for empowering women, Dr. Pelz has built a body of work that is as accessible as it is transformative. This cookbook is based on her approach, which combines short, effective meal preparation with nutrition aimed at supporting hormones, sustaining energy, and promoting a healthy metabolism. Here, we'll delve into the philosophy behind the 10-Minute Pelz Diet, explore the importance of hormone health for women over 40, and introduce the concepts that make this cookbook a practical guide for achieving sustainable wellness.

Who is Dr. Mindy Pelz?

Dr. Mindy Pelz, DC, is a recognized thought leader in functional and holistic medicine, focusing particularly on women's health. With over two decades of experience in clinical practice, Dr. Pelz has dedicated her career to helping individuals understand how to manage their health naturally. Her work emphasizes addressing the root causes of health issues rather than relying solely on medication, which has resonated with countless women seeking non-invasive solutions. Her expertise spans a range of subjects including hormone health, intermittent fasting, and gut health, areas that are especially significant for women in their 40s, 50s, and beyond.

Her books, online courses, and social media presence have garnered a large following, particularly among women interested in alternative approaches to hormone balance and metabolic health. Dr. Pelz's focus on science-backed strategies for managing hormones has inspired a community of women to take control of their wellness journey in ways that feel intuitive and achievable.

The 10-Minute Pelz Diet reflects her commitment to making health accessible, practical, and effective. The principles in this book are inspired by her teachings on the benefits of intermittent fasting, gut health optimization, and hormone support, adapted to fit into a busy lifestyle with quick recipes that don't require hours of prep or hard-to-find ingredients.

The Philosophy Behind the 10-Minute Pelz Diet

The 10-Minute Pelz Diet is based on the idea that creating a healthy lifestyle should be straightforward and sustainable. Many women over 40 face challenges such as fluctuating hormones, shifts in metabolism, and new lifestyle demands that make traditional diet approaches less effective. Dr. Pelz believes that a diet plan should fit seamlessly into one's life rather than disrupt it. The emphasis on quick, nutrient-dense meals allows women to incorporate the principles of hormone balance and metabolic health without sacrificing their time or energy.

Dr. Pelz's approach rests on five core principles that set her diet apart:

1. **Simplicity**: The diet is built around meals that can be prepared in 10 minutes or less, making it accessible for women with busy schedules. The quick recipes are designed to provide nutrient-rich meals that cater to hormonal needs, supporting energy and metabolism without unnecessary complexity.

2. **Hormone Support**: Hormonal changes are a significant factor in women's health over 40, influencing everything from weight gain to mood swings. This diet includes ingredients that help stabilize hormones, balancing blood sugar, and managing inflammation, which are all essential for hormone health.

3. **Gut Health Focus**: Dr. Pelz emphasizes the importance of gut health as a cornerstone of overall wellness, particularly for women in midlife. By including fiber-rich, probiotic, and anti-inflammatory foods, the diet helps improve digestion, enhance nutrient absorption, and reduce bloating—a common issue for women over 40.

4. **Intermittent Fasting Compatibility**: The 10-Minute Pelz Diet is designed to complement intermittent fasting, a practice that has shown significant benefits for hormone balance and metabolism. The recipes are low in refined sugars and high in nutrients, making them ideal for breaking a fast while keeping blood sugar levels stable.

5. **Long-Term Wellness**: Unlike quick-fix diets that focus on restrictive calorie counts or unsustainable meal plans, this diet promotes gradual, lasting change. It prioritizes balance, empowering women to make nutritional choices that lead to sustainable wellness and a better quality of life.

The goal of this cookbook is not just to provide recipes but to offer a complete approach to wellness that supports women through the unique hormonal changes they face as they age. By understanding the role of diet in hormone balance, energy, and metabolism, readers can use these recipes as tools to enhance their health in meaningful ways.

Why Hormone Health Matters for Women Over 40

Hormones play a vital role in how women feel, look, and function, influencing everything from energy levels to weight management, mood, and even skin health. After age 40, women experience shifts in estrogen, progesterone, and testosterone levels as they approach perimenopause and menopause. These hormonal fluctuations can lead to symptoms like weight gain, fatigue, hot flashes, mood swings, and sleep disturbances.

In traditional medicine, these symptoms are often treated with hormone replacement therapy (HRT) or medications, which can be effective but also come with potential side effects. Dr. Pelz's philosophy is that lifestyle changes—especially through diet—can make a significant difference in managing these symptoms. By focusing on hormone-supportive foods and reducing dietary triggers that exacerbate imbalances, women can help regulate their hormones naturally.

Incorporating hormone-friendly nutrients into meals can reduce symptoms associated with menopause and perimenopause, such as:

➢ **Phytoestrogens**: Found in foods like flaxseeds and soy, phytoestrogens mimic estrogen in the body and may help balance low estrogen levels, a common issue during menopause.
➢ **Healthy Fats**: Sources like avocados, nuts, and olive oil are essential for hormone production, helping stabilize moods and providing steady energy.
➢ **Cruciferous Vegetables**: Vegetables like broccoli, kale, and cauliflower are rich in compounds that support estrogen metabolism, aiding the body in processing excess estrogen and balancing hormones.

By including these ingredients in quick, easy recipes, the 10-Minute Pelz Diet aims to make hormone balance achievable on a daily basis.

Key Principles of the 10-Minute Pelz Diet for Sustainable Weight Loss, Energy, and Hormone Balance

The 10-Minute Pelz Diet isn't just about quick recipes; it's about making mindful choices that support the body's needs, especially as it undergoes age-related changes. Here are some of the core principles that set this diet apart as a practical, long-term solution for women's health:

➤ **Low Glycemic Index Foods**: Meals are focused on low glycemic ingredients that prevent blood sugar spikes, reducing cravings and stabilizing energy levels. Managing blood sugar is crucial for women over 40, as insulin resistance can increase with age, leading to fatigue and weight gain.

➤ **High Nutrient Density**: Since metabolism can slow with age, every meal in the diet is packed with vitamins, minerals, and antioxidants. These nutrient-dense meals ensure that each calorie contributes to energy, tissue repair, and overall vitality, rather than empty calories that offer little nutritional value.

➤ **Protein Prioritization**: Protein supports muscle maintenance and keeps the metabolism active. The diet incorporates lean proteins from plant and animal sources to ensure a balance that is both filling and supportive of muscle mass, which naturally declines with age.

➤ **Anti-Inflammatory Foods**: Ingredients like turmeric, ginger, and leafy greens combat inflammation, which can worsen symptoms of hormonal imbalance. Chronic inflammation has been linked to a range of health issues, from joint pain to heart disease, and this diet includes foods known to have anti-inflammatory properties.

➤ **Fasting-Friendly Options**: By including nutrient-rich, low-calorie recipes, the diet supports fasting without compromising nutrition. This makes it easy for women to combine intermittent fasting with balanced meals that sustain energy and hormone health.

These principles make the 10-Minute Pelz Diet a lifestyle shift rather than a temporary diet. It provides a structure that allows women to eat intuitively while incorporating nutrient-packed, hormone-friendly foods that fit into any schedule.

The Role of Fasting and Gut Health in The 10-Minute Pelz Diet

Fasting and gut health are two pillars of the 10-Minute Pelz Diet, contributing to its effectiveness in promoting lasting wellness. Both are backed by research showing their benefits for hormone health, metabolic stability, and energy levels.

Fasting for Hormone and Metabolic Health

Intermittent fasting has gained popularity as a tool for managing weight, but its benefits go beyond the scale. Dr. Pelz advocates for fasting because it allows the body to rest, digest, and enter a state of repair. Fasting has been shown to:

➢ **Stabilize Blood Sugar**: By reducing the frequency of meals, fasting gives the body time to regulate insulin, which can prevent the blood sugar highs and lows that lead to fatigue and cravings.

➢ **Support Growth Hormone**: Fasting boosts growth hormone production, which is crucial for metabolism and muscle health, especially as natural levels decline with age.

➢ **Enhance Autophagy**: This process involves cellular repair, where the body cleans out damaged cells and regenerates new ones. Autophagy is beneficial for overall longevity and is particularly valuable for reducing inflammation, which can worsen with hormonal changes.

Women over 40 can particularly benefit from fasting because it supports metabolic flexibility, making it easier to switch from burning glucose to burning fat for energy. This is essential for managing weight and energy levels effectively.

Gut Health for Overall Wellness

The gut is often referred to as the "second brain," influencing everything from mood to immunity and, importantly, hormone health. Dr. Pelz's diet includes foods that support a healthy gut microbiome, focusing on prebiotics (fiber that feeds beneficial bacteria) and probiotics (foods that introduce good bacteria).

A healthy gut:

➢ **Improves Nutrient Absorption**: With age, nutrient absorption can decline, but a healthy gut ensures that the body is getting the most out of every meal.

➢ **Supports Hormone Regulation**: Certain gut bacteria are involved in metabolizing estrogen, and a balanced microbiome aids in regulating hormone levels, reducing the likelihood of imbalances.

➢ **Reduces Inflammation**: Gut health is closely linked to systemic inflammation, and a balanced gut can help reduce inflammatory markers that may worsen hormonal symptoms.

By combining gut-friendly ingredients with intermittent fasting, the 10-Minute Pelz Diet enhances digestion, supports hormone health, and promotes lasting energy.

The Journey Ahead with The 10-Minute Pelz Diet Cookbook

As we dive into the recipes in this cookbook, remember that each one is crafted with the unique needs of women over 40 in mind. Whether you're looking for quick meal solutions to balance hormones, boost energy, or lose weight sustainably, these recipes are designed to be flexible, nourishing, and delicious. Inspired by Dr. Mindy Pelz's approach, this cookbook is here to empower you with the tools you need to make wellness an achievable part of everyday life.

With each recipe, you're taking a step toward greater control over your health, harnessing the power of simple, nutritious meals that support you through hormonal changes and beyond. Enjoy the journey, and savor the simplicity and effectiveness of the 10-Minute Pelz Diet.

How to Use This Cookbook

The *10-Minute Pelz Diet Cookbook* is designed to bring healthy eating into reach for busy women, making meal prep straightforward, satisfying, and effective. Inspired by Dr. Mindy Pelz's research and philosophy on hormone health, energy optimization, and weight management, this cookbook organizes over 150 recipes to help you create balanced, nutrient-dense meals in just minutes. It serves as a practical guide for navigating hormonal changes, improving gut health, and maintaining a steady weight—all through the power of nutrition. Whether you're new to Dr. Pelz's approach or familiar with her work, this guide provides the roadmap for using the cookbook in a way that enhances your health and simplifies your life.

The Structure of the Cookbook

The *10-Minute Pelz Diet Cookbook* is organized into chapters that correspond to specific wellness goals, each one carefully selected to address women's unique health needs during midlife. You'll find five core chapters, each dedicated to a different wellness focus—hormone balance, energy support, sustainable weight loss, gut health, and anti-inflammatory benefits. Within each chapter, breakfast, lunch, and dinner recipes are grouped to allow easy mixing and matching according to your daily schedule, energy needs, and cravings.

Each chapter includes a section called "Fasting Tips" or "Gut Health Tips," with insights on incorporating these practices into your routine. These sections support the core themes of Dr. Pelz's work and offer strategies to make the most of each meal's benefits. These tips ensure that the meals aren't just nourishing but also deeply restorative, supporting your journey toward optimal health.

Setting Up Your Kitchen for Quick, Easy Meals

A successful journey with this cookbook starts with a well-equipped kitchen. You don't need specialized appliances or gadgets; just a few essential tools can help streamline meal prep, making it easier to achieve the quick and healthy meal prep Dr. Pelz advocates.

A high-speed blender will prove invaluable for preparing smoothies, sauces, and soups that add flavor, nutrients, and variety. For quick prep, a good quality knife and cutting board make it easy to chop vegetables, fruits, and proteins quickly. To prepare the many stovetop-based meals, a nonstick or stainless steel skillet can handle stir-fries and one-pan dishes. A small saucepan will be useful for oatmeal, quick soups, and sauces, while a salad spinner speeds up the preparation of salads by allowing you to rinse and dry greens quickly. Though not necessary, a food processor can help with chopping vegetables and creating sauces or dressings, saving valuable time. For accuracy and balance in flavors, have a set of measuring cups and spoons on hand.

Stocking your pantry with a few versatile staples will make it easy to follow recipes without multiple trips to the store. High-quality oils like olive, avocado, and coconut oil provide the healthy fats crucial for hormone support. Keep a variety of nuts and seeds on hand, such as almonds, chia seeds, flaxseeds, and pumpkin seeds, which add texture, protein, and nutrients, especially in hormone-supportive recipes. Whole grains like quinoa, brown rice, and oats provide complex carbohydrates that contribute to energy and satiety. Plant-based proteins like canned beans, lentils, and chickpeas offer a nutritious and fiber-rich source of protein, essential for supporting gut health and hormone balance. Dried herbs and spices like turmeric, ginger, cinnamon, and garlic powder will add flavor and anti-inflammatory properties, while broths (bone broth and vegetable broth) enrich soups with depth of flavor and nutrients. Finally, vinegars and citrus, such as apple cider vinegar and lemon, add brightness to dishes and support digestion.

Tailoring Recipes to Your Health Goals

One of the strengths of the *10-Minute Pelz Diet Cookbook* is its flexibility, allowing you to adapt recipes to fit your unique wellness goals. Whether your main focus is balancing hormones, maintaining steady energy, managing weight, or improving gut health, each chapter provides tailored recipes that align with these goals.

For those focusing on hormone health, Chapter 1 offers meals that prioritize hormone-stabilizing ingredients. Leafy greens, flaxseeds, cruciferous vegetables, and healthy fats—such as avocado and olive oil—support the endocrine system. These foods help stabilize levels of estrogen and progesterone, essential hormones for women's health in midlife. When aiming for hormone balance, try combining the Hormone-Balancing Avocado & Berry Smoothie for breakfast, Kale & Sweet Potato Hormone Salad for lunch, and Wild-Caught Salmon with Roasted Asparagus for dinner. These recipes, when combined, ensure a day filled with hormone-supporting nutrients.

If energy support is a priority, Chapter 2 offers a wealth of meals focused on balanced macronutrients, with a mix of complex carbohydrates, protein, and healthy fats. This balance is designed to prevent energy crashes and promote sustained stamina, making them ideal for overcoming afternoon slumps or morning fatigue. For a full day of energy-boosting meals, you might start with an Almond Butter & Banana Smoothie in the morning, followed by a Quinoa & Black Bean Salad for lunch, and Garlic Shrimp with Cauliflower Rice for dinner.

When sustainable weight loss is your goal, Chapter 3 includes low-calorie, high-nutrient recipes that keep you satisfied without adding unnecessary calories. By focusing on meals that regulate blood sugar levels and reduce cravings, you'll have the tools to manage weight sustainably and avoid the pitfalls of restrictive dieting. A full day of weight management meals might include a Low-Calorie Berry & Almond Smoothie for breakfast, Turkey Lettuce Wraps with Veggies for lunch, and Grilled Lemon Chicken with Steamed Broccoli for dinner.

For those focused on gut health, Chapter 4 provides recipes rich in prebiotics, probiotics, and fiber, essential for a balanced microbiome. These meals support digestion, reduce bloating, and improve nutrient absorption. For a gut health-focused day, start with the Probiotic Greek Yogurt & Berries Bowl, enjoy a Kimchi & Cabbage Salad with Sesame Dressing for lunch, and end with Probiotic-Rich Salmon with Sauerkraut for dinner.

Finally, if anti-inflammatory benefits are top of mind, Chapter 5 includes meals with ingredients like turmeric, ginger, and leafy greens, all known for their anti-inflammatory properties. Chronic inflammation can contribute to hormonal imbalances, weight gain, and fatigue, so reducing it is key for a healthier lifestyle. For a day focused on inflammation reduction, try the Anti-Inflammatory Golden Milk Smoothie for breakfast, Carrot & Ginger Anti-Inflammatory Soup for lunch, and Baked Salmon with Turmeric & Lemon for dinner.

Making the Most of Fasting and Meal Timing

The *10-Minute Pelz Diet Cookbook* is designed to be compatible with intermittent fasting, a practice that Dr. Pelz supports for its benefits in hormone regulation, metabolic flexibility, and energy stabilization. Integrating these recipes into a fasting routine can further enhance their effectiveness, especially when you pay attention to the timing and type of meals you eat when breaking a fast.

If fasting is part of your routine, choose nutrient-dense meals to break your fast, focusing on a balance of protein, fats, and fiber, as these will provide lasting energy and prevent blood sugar spikes. The Probiotic Greek Yogurt & Berries Bowl or Protein-Packed Cottage Cheese & Berry Bowl are ideal for breaking a fast as they offer the right combination of nutrients to stabilize your blood sugar and keep you satisfied for hours. Alternatively, the Sautéed Greens & Sweet Potato Bowl is another excellent option for breaking a fast while still getting in a hefty dose of fiber and essential nutrients.

In terms of timing, many women over 40 find that fasting for 14 to 16 hours works well, allowing them to eat within a 10- to 8-hour window. This schedule not only gives the digestive system time to rest but also helps stabilize insulin levels, which is particularly beneficial for hormonal balance and metabolic health. Within this eating window, you can easily incorporate breakfast, lunch, and dinner recipes that support your specific wellness goals, tailoring each meal to keep you energized and satisfied.

If you prefer a more flexible fasting schedule, focus on starting your day with a light meal or smoothie and transitioning to more substantial meals as the day progresses. The recipes in this cookbook are designed to be adaptable, so you can adjust the portions or swap ingredients based on your preferences, allowing you to enjoy the meals on both fasting and non-fasting days.

Building a Sustainable Routine with the 10-Minute Pelz Diet

The *10-Minute Pelz Diet Cookbook* is more than a collection of recipes; it's a guide for creating a healthy, sustainable lifestyle. One of the core principles behind Dr. Pelz's approach is that a healthy diet should fit seamlessly into your life, not demand drastic changes or complex meal prep. By keeping meals simple, nutritious, and quick to prepare, this cookbook empowers you to make better food choices consistently, even on the busiest days.

To build a routine that works for you, consider planning your meals at the start of each week, identifying recipes that fit your current goals. If hormone health is your focus, build your meals around recipes in Chapter 1. If you're looking to manage weight, try integrating more meals from Chapter 3 into your week. The flexibility of the recipes means that you don't have to stick to a single chapter—you can create your own combination of meals from each chapter to suit your needs.

As you start using the cookbook, pay attention to how different meals make you feel. You may find that energy-boosting breakfasts help set a positive tone for your day or that anti-inflammatory dinners make it easier to wind down and rest. By tuning into how your body responds, you'll gain valuable insights into which meals support your unique needs and preferences.

Remember, the goal of the *10-Minute Pelz Diet* isn't to follow a rigid plan but to create a routine that nourishes your body, supports your wellness goals, and aligns with your lifestyle. As you experiment with different recipes and adapt the cookbook to your needs, you'll be taking important steps toward lasting health, one 10-minute meal at a time.

The Role of Fasting in Hormone Health

Fasting has become more than just a wellness trend; it's now recognized as a powerful tool for supporting hormone health, particularly for women over 40. Unlike diets that require constant calorie restriction, fasting offers a flexible, science-backed approach that supports the body's natural processes. For women facing hormonal shifts due to perimenopause, menopause, and aging, intermittent fasting can provide relief from common symptoms like weight gain, fatigue, mood swings, and low energy. This chapter delves into the role of fasting in hormone health, explains how it works on a biological level, and offers practical insights into integrating fasting effectively and safely.

How Fasting Affects Hormones

Hormones are chemical messengers that regulate almost every function in the body, from metabolism and energy levels to mood and digestion. As women age, hormonal levels begin to fluctuate, particularly estrogen and progesterone, which can lead to issues such as weight gain, fatigue, and sleep disturbances. Fasting can help by promoting hormonal balance and enhancing the body's ability to regulate insulin, cortisol, and even growth hormones, all of which are crucial for maintaining energy and overall wellness.

Fasting triggers changes in the body's metabolism, one of the most significant being insulin sensitivity. When you fast, your body doesn't have a constant supply of glucose to burn, so it turns to stored fat for energy. This process helps improve insulin sensitivity, allowing cells to absorb glucose more effectively and stabilize blood sugar levels. For women, particularly those in midlife, this reduction in insulin levels can lead to better energy levels, reduced cravings, and more stable moods throughout the day.

Moreover, fasting has been shown to reduce cortisol levels over time, which can lower chronic stress. Cortisol, commonly known as the stress hormone, tends to be higher in women as they age, especially during perimenopause and menopause. By regulating cortisol through fasting, you may find it easier to manage stress, which, in turn, supports other hormone systems in the body, promoting better sleep, mental clarity, and even digestion.

In addition to insulin and cortisol, fasting also influences growth hormone levels, which play a key role in cell repair, metabolism, and muscle maintenance. Growth hormone levels decline with age, but fasting can help boost their production, especially during the fasting window. This is beneficial for maintaining lean muscle mass, supporting a healthy metabolism, and promoting cellular repair—all crucial aspects of healthy aging.

Benefits of Fasting for Women Over 40

For women in their 40s and beyond, the hormonal landscape changes drastically, bringing new challenges that fasting can help address. Weight gain, often due to hormonal shifts, is a common concern, and fasting can aid in weight management by improving metabolic efficiency and encouraging fat burning. Fasting promotes autophagy, a process where the body cleans out damaged cells and regenerates healthier ones. This process not only boosts metabolism but also helps reduce inflammation, which can be a significant contributor to weight gain and fatigue in midlife.

Fasting also has benefits for cognitive health. Many women experience "brain fog" as they go through menopause, and fasting helps improve mental clarity by stabilizing blood sugar and enhancing ketone production. Ketones, an alternative energy source produced by the liver during fasting, are known to cross the blood-brain barrier, providing the brain with a steady source of energy and improving focus and cognitive function.

Beyond weight management and mental clarity, fasting can also help regulate reproductive hormones, including estrogen. During menopause, estrogen levels drop, leading to symptoms like hot flashes, mood swings, and insomnia. By improving insulin sensitivity, fasting helps balance these hormonal fluctuations, creating a more stable internal environment. Additionally, studies suggest that fasting may help improve progesterone levels, which tend to drop significantly during menopause, leading to better mood regulation and reduced irritability.

Types of Fasting and Their Effects on Hormones

There are several methods of fasting, but not all of them are equally beneficial for hormone health, especially for women. The most popular forms include time-restricted eating, the 16:8 method, and 24-hour fasting. Each has unique benefits and effects on hormone regulation, allowing you to choose the best approach based on your lifestyle and hormonal needs.

Time-restricted eating involves eating within a specific window each day, such as 12 hours of fasting and 12 hours of eating. This method is gentle on the body, making it an ideal starting point for women new to fasting. By extending the fasting window to 14 or 16 hours (as in the 16:8 method), you can enhance the benefits of fat burning and metabolic regulation, promoting hormonal balance.

The 16:8 method, where you fast for 16 hours and eat within an 8-hour window, is one of the most widely used forms of intermittent fasting. This schedule helps improve insulin sensitivity and supports metabolic flexibility, allowing the body to burn fat for fuel more efficiently. Many women find the 16:8 method manageable and effective for weight management, energy, and reducing symptoms of hormonal imbalance.

For women experienced with fasting, a 24-hour fast once a week or every two weeks may offer additional benefits. A full 24-hour fast allows the body to enter a deeper state of autophagy, which supports cellular repair and reduces inflammation. However, this method may be too intense for some women, especially those sensitive to blood sugar fluctuations or those dealing with high stress levels. Listening to your body is crucial, as prolonged fasting may not be suitable for everyone and can sometimes lead to fatigue if done excessively.

How to Begin Fasting Safely

Starting a fasting routine can seem daunting, especially if you're new to the practice, but the key is to begin gradually and listen to your body's needs. Start by delaying your breakfast by an hour or two to gently extend your fasting window. Over time, as your body adjusts, you can gradually increase the fasting period. This approach makes it easier to adapt to fasting without experiencing intense hunger or energy dips.

Hydration is essential when fasting. Drinking water, herbal tea, and even adding a bit of sea salt can help prevent dehydration and support electrolyte balance. Many women find that drinking herbal teas or adding lemon to water helps curb hunger pangs, making it easier to go longer between meals.

When you're ready to break your fast, prioritize a nutrient-dense meal that includes protein, healthy fats, and fiber. This combination will help stabilize blood sugar levels and prevent cravings later in the day. Good options include a yogurt and berry parfait with nuts or a bowl of oatmeal with chia seeds, almond butter, and fresh berries. These meals support hormone health and keep you feeling full and energized.

The most important thing to remember is that fasting should feel sustainable and supportive, not restrictive. If you experience dizziness, irritability, or extreme hunger, consider shortening your fasting window or adding in a small, balanced snack. The goal is to work with your body, not against it, allowing fasting to become an enjoyable part of your routine.

Common Challenges and How to Overcome Them

Many women find that the first few weeks of fasting come with challenges, from hunger pangs to mental fatigue. Fortunately, these effects are usually temporary as the body adapts to using stored energy. One common challenge is managing hunger, especially during the first few days. Hunger often comes in waves, so drinking water, herbal tea, or coffee (without sugar or milk) can help ease this sensation. If hunger persists, try including more protein and fiber in your meals, as these macronutrients keep you fuller for longer and reduce cravings.

Energy dips are another common concern, particularly if you're new to fasting. These dips may occur as your body shifts from burning glucose to using fat for energy. To manage this, prioritize balanced meals within your eating window, and consider starting with shorter fasting periods, such as a 12-hour fast, until your body adjusts.

Social situations can also be challenging when fasting, especially during gatherings that involve food. Planning ahead can help; try to schedule your fasting window around events or bring a small, healthy snack if you're unsure of the food options available. Remember, it's okay to adjust your fasting schedule occasionally to accommodate social events without feeling guilty.

Finally, listening to your body is essential, especially when facing physical stress, illness, or high levels of fatigue. Fasting should be a tool for health, not a rigid requirement, so if there are days when fasting feels too demanding, give yourself permission to eat according to your needs.

Integrating Fasting with the 10-Minute Pelz Diet

The *10-Minute Pelz Diet Cookbook* is specifically designed to complement a fasting lifestyle. Each recipe in the cookbook focuses on quick, nutrient-dense meals that align with Dr. Pelz's principles of hormone health, energy stability, and metabolic support. Many of the meals in this cookbook are perfect for breaking a fast, as they provide the right balance of macronutrients without overwhelming the digestive system.

When planning meals around fasting, focus on recipes that stabilize blood sugar and provide sustained energy. Smoothies, salads, and light soups are excellent options for breaking a fast. For example, a berry smoothie with almond milk and chia seeds or a mixed greens salad with grilled salmon, avocado, and pumpkin seeds are ideal post-fast meals, as they are easy to digest and loaded with fiber, healthy fats, and protein.

Combining fasting with the recipes in this book allows you to reap the benefits of both practices without the strain of extended meal prep. The flexibility of the 10-minute recipes means you can quickly prepare balanced meals, even after a long fast, ensuring that you nourish your body without feeling restricted.

Embracing Fasting as Part of a Sustainable Lifestyle

Fasting can be a transformative practice for women over 40, providing numerous benefits for hormone health, weight management, mental clarity, and more. By integrating fasting with the 10-Minute Pelz Diet, you create a lifestyle that is not only sustainable but also deeply supportive of the body's changing needs. Fasting doesn't have to be a strict regimen; it can be an adaptable, enjoyable practice that enhances your relationship with food and health.

As you experiment with fasting, remember that the journey is about finding what works best for your body. Over time, fasting can become a natural and nourishing part of your daily routine, providing a powerful foundation for hormonal health and overall wellness.

Gut Health for Women Over 40: Why It Matters

As women enter their 40s and beyond, their bodies undergo several transformative changes that affect not only hormonal health but also gut health. The gut, often called the "second brain," plays a pivotal role in maintaining physical, mental, and emotional wellness. For women over 40, gut health is more than just a digestive concern; it's an essential component of overall vitality, influencing everything from energy levels and immune function to skin health, mood, and hormone balance.

This chapter explores the importance of gut health for women in midlife, explaining why it matters, how it interacts with other systems, and ways to support a thriving gut ecosystem for better health outcomes. By understanding the unique relationship between gut health and women's wellness, you'll be better equipped to make informed choices that benefit your digestive system, balance hormones, and promote long-lasting well-being.

Understanding the Gut Microbiome and Its Functions

The gut microbiome is a complex network of trillions of bacteria, viruses, and fungi that reside primarily in the large intestine. These microorganisms aren't just passive residents; they actively contribute to bodily processes, breaking down food, synthesizing essential nutrients, and communicating with other organs through chemical signals. In a balanced state, the microbiome helps protect against harmful pathogens, supports nutrient absorption, and plays a vital role in maintaining immune health.

Women's gut health, in particular, is intricately linked to hormone regulation. Many of the bacteria in the gut contribute to metabolizing and detoxifying hormones like estrogen. When the gut microbiome is balanced and functioning well, it effectively breaks down and removes excess hormones from the body, preventing hormonal imbalances. Conversely, an unhealthy or imbalanced microbiome, often termed "dysbiosis," can lead to various health issues, including bloating, fatigue, digestive discomfort, and even mood disturbances.

In addition to digestion and hormone metabolism, the gut microbiome influences the production of neurotransmitters, such as serotonin, which regulates mood and sleep. Roughly 90% of serotonin, a "feel-good" hormone, is produced in the gut. This connection between gut health and mental health is significant, as many women over 40 experience shifts in mood and energy that are often attributed solely to hormonal changes. Improving gut health can provide a more holistic solution to these challenges, supporting both mental and physical wellness.

Why Gut Health Becomes More Important After 40

After age 40, women face a natural decline in estrogen and progesterone levels, two hormones crucial to various aspects of health. Estrogen, in particular, has a protective effect on gut health by promoting a diverse and balanced microbiome. As estrogen levels decrease, the diversity of gut bacteria may also decline, increasing the risk of dysbiosis. A less diverse microbiome can lead to inflammation, weight gain, and metabolic issues, all of which are common concerns for women in midlife.

In addition to hormonal changes, aging can affect the body's natural digestive processes. The production of digestive enzymes tends to decrease, which can make it more difficult to break down certain foods, leading to bloating, gas, and nutrient malabsorption. Many women also experience a slowing metabolism as they age, which can contribute to unwanted weight gain. A healthy gut supports metabolic efficiency by enhancing nutrient absorption and promoting balanced blood sugar levels, which are essential for maintaining a healthy weight.

Gut health also becomes crucial for immune function as women age. The gut houses about 70% of the immune system, making it a primary defense against infections and illnesses. A robust gut microbiome strengthens the immune system, helping the body resist pathogens and reducing chronic inflammation. This is particularly valuable for women over 40, as inflammation and immune resilience become increasingly important factors in overall health.

The Connection Between Gut Health and Hormones

The gut is often referred to as the body's "hormone helper" because of its direct involvement in hormone metabolism and regulation. In women over 40, gut health plays a particularly vital role in managing estrogen levels. The gut-liver axis, a biochemical pathway that involves both the liver and gut, is responsible for processing and eliminating estrogen from the body. When the gut microbiome is balanced and diverse, it supports this detoxification process by breaking down excess estrogen and ensuring it is safely excreted.

In cases of dysbiosis, however, certain gut bacteria produce an enzyme called beta-glucuronidase, which can cause reabsorption of estrogen into the bloodstream. This reabsorption can lead to an excess of estrogen, which is linked to various hormonal imbalances and symptoms, including weight gain, mood swings, bloating, and irregular menstrual cycles. For women experiencing perimenopause and menopause, managing estrogen levels is essential, and supporting gut health is one of the most effective ways to maintain hormonal balance naturally.

The gut also interacts with the adrenal glands, which produce cortisol, the primary stress hormone. Chronic stress can disrupt gut health, and in turn, an unhealthy gut can lead to increased cortisol production, creating a cycle that negatively impacts mental health and energy levels. This connection between gut health and cortisol is significant for women over 40, as stress management becomes more critical with age.

Signs of an Unhealthy Gut

Understanding the signs of an unhealthy gut is the first step toward restoring balance. Many of the symptoms of poor gut health are subtle or easily attributed to other factors, which can make it difficult to recognize the underlying issue. Some of the common signs of an unhealthy gut include:

➤ **Digestive Discomfort**: Frequent bloating, gas, constipation, or diarrhea are often signs that the gut microbiome is out of balance.
➤ **Frequent Illness**: A compromised gut weakens the immune system, making the body more susceptible to colds, infections, and other illnesses.
➤ **Unexplained Fatigue**: If you feel tired or sluggish despite getting enough rest, it may be due to poor gut health affecting nutrient absorption and energy production.
➤ **Mood Swings and Anxiety**: The gut-brain axis means that an imbalanced gut can affect mental health, leading to symptoms like irritability, anxiety, and depression.
➤ **Skin Issues**: Conditions like eczema, acne, and rosacea can often be traced back to gut health issues, as the gut microbiome influences skin inflammation and hydration.
➤ **Food Sensitivities**: A leaky or inflamed gut lining can increase sensitivity to certain foods, causing reactions such as bloating, headaches, or digestive discomfort.

If you experience any of these symptoms regularly, addressing your gut health may help alleviate them and improve your overall well-being.

Tips for Supporting Gut Health in Midlife

Supporting gut health doesn't require an extreme diet overhaul but rather a few key lifestyle changes that can help promote a balanced microbiome. Small adjustments to your diet and routine can make a significant difference, especially when it comes to balancing hormones, improving digestion, and enhancing mood and energy.

One of the most important steps is increasing fiber intake, particularly from plant-based sources. Fiber serves as a prebiotic, feeding beneficial bacteria and encouraging the growth of a diverse microbiome. Fruits, vegetables, whole grains, and legumes are excellent sources of fiber that also provide a wide range of vitamins and minerals. Fiber not only supports gut health but also aids in regulating blood sugar and cholesterol levels.

Incorporating probiotic-rich foods into your diet can also support a healthy microbiome. Fermented foods like yogurt, kefir, sauerkraut, kimchi, and miso contain live bacteria that add beneficial microbes to your gut. These foods are particularly helpful for maintaining gut health, especially if you're experiencing digestive discomfort or hormonal imbalances.

Hydration is another essential factor for gut health. Drinking plenty of water supports digestion and helps prevent constipation, a common issue that can worsen with age. Water also assists in the elimination of toxins and excess hormones from the body, ensuring that your digestive system functions smoothly.

Finally, managing stress is crucial for maintaining a healthy gut. Chronic stress disrupts the gut-brain axis, contributing to dysbiosis and inflammation. Incorporating stress-relieving practices, such as meditation, deep breathing exercises, or regular physical activity, can help maintain a balanced microbiome and reduce the risk of stress-induced gut issues.

Integrating Gut Health Practices with the 10-Minute Pelz Diet

The *10-Minute Pelz Diet* aligns well with practices that support gut health. Each recipe is crafted with high-fiber, whole-food ingredients, and many include gut-friendly options like yogurt, greens, and fibrous vegetables. The meals in this cookbook are designed to be easy on the digestive system, providing the essential nutrients needed for a thriving microbiome without heavy or hard-to-digest ingredients.

To maximize gut health benefits, try including at least one high-fiber or probiotic-rich food with each meal. Starting the day with a breakfast smoothie that includes chia seeds or flaxseeds can help feed your gut bacteria. Lunchtime salads featuring leafy greens, raw vegetables, and fermented foods are also excellent choices for gut health. For dinner, soups and stews with a variety of vegetables and a bone broth base provide nourishing support for the gut lining, especially if you struggle with digestion in the evenings.

Combining these meals with mindful eating practices can also support gut health. Chewing food thoroughly, eating slowly, and focusing on your meal can enhance digestion and prevent discomfort. Mindful eating not only improves nutrient absorption but also helps you tune into your body's hunger and fullness signals, creating a more intuitive approach to eating.

Creating a Routine That Supports Long-Term Gut Health

Achieving and maintaining good gut health is not a one-time effort but an ongoing commitment to balanced, mindful eating. Building a routine around gut health doesn't mean restricting your diet or making drastic changes; instead, it involves small, sustainable habits that support a balanced microbiome over time.

Try setting aside time each week to prepare gut-friendly foods, such as a batch of yogurt parfaits, chopped vegetables, or fermented foods like sauerkraut. Keeping these items ready to go can make it easier to incorporate them into your meals without adding extra preparation time.

Consistency is key when it comes to gut health. By regularly including high-fiber, fermented, and nutrient-dense foods in your diet, you can create a stable environment for beneficial bacteria to thrive. Over time, these small, intentional choices can improve digestion, boost immune health, and create a foundation for long-term wellness.

For women over 40, taking care of gut health means much more than simply avoiding digestive issues. A balanced, diverse microbiome has a ripple effect, influencing everything from hormone levels and immune resilience to mental clarity and energy. With the guidance and recipes provided in the *10-Minute Pelz Diet Cookbook*, supporting your gut health becomes an accessible, enjoyable part of your wellness routine, empowering you to navigate midlife with vitality and confidence.

Meal Planning for Busy Women: 10-Minute Recipes for Daily Success

Finding time for healthy cooking can be challenging, especially for women balancing the demands of a busy schedule with the need to eat well. The *10-Minute Pelz Diet Cookbook* was created with this reality in mind, delivering a selection of nutrient-dense recipes that fit seamlessly into the most hectic of days. By using simple ingredients, streamlined cooking techniques, and Dr. Mindy Pelz's health-focused philosophy, this cookbook allows you to prepare meals that support energy, hormone balance, and gut health without spending hours in the kitchen.

This chapter covers essential meal-planning strategies tailored for busy women, practical tips for setting up a time-efficient kitchen, and guidelines on using the 10-minute recipes to build a daily routine that aligns with your wellness goals.

The Power of Meal Planning for Women Over 40

Meal planning is more than just an efficiency tool—it's a powerful way to ensure that your nutritional needs are met consistently. For women over 40, hormonal shifts, metabolic changes, and fluctuations in energy levels can make healthy eating essential for feeling and functioning at your best. By planning meals in advance, you reduce decision fatigue, curb last-minute unhealthy choices, and prioritize nutrient-rich foods that support your body's changing needs.

Thoughtful meal planning can also help you achieve specific health goals. Whether you're focusing on hormone balance, weight management, or gut health, each recipe in this cookbook is tailored to address these needs in some way. Meal planning allows you to align your diet with these goals, creating a rhythm that fuels your body and mind.

Getting Started: Essentials for Quick and Efficient Meal Prep

The key to making meal prep both manageable and enjoyable is a well-organized kitchen. A few basic tools and a well-stocked pantry can make all the difference in how quickly you can get meals on the table.

Begin with essential kitchen tools like a high-speed blender for smoothies and sauces, a sharp knife and cutting board for quick prep, and a large skillet or sauté pan for one-pan meals. These tools are not only versatile but also allow for easy cleanup, making meal prep feel less like a chore and more like a routine you look forward to. Other helpful tools include a salad spinner to rinse and dry greens quickly, a small saucepan for oats or soups, and a food processor for chopping vegetables or preparing dressings.

Stocking your pantry with versatile, nutrient-dense ingredients is also crucial. Having items like olive oil, nuts, seeds, canned beans, whole grains, and dried herbs and spices on hand allows you to prepare balanced meals without multiple trips to the store. Keeping ingredients that align with your health goals, such as fiber-rich grains for gut health, anti-inflammatory spices for hormone balance, and high-quality proteins for sustained energy, simplifies the planning process and provides endless meal options.

Building a Weekly Meal Plan with 10-Minute Recipes

Creating a weekly meal plan doesn't have to be rigid or overwhelming. In fact, the *10-Minute Pelz Diet Cookbook* is designed to make meal planning flexible and enjoyable, allowing you to mix and match recipes based on your personal preferences, schedule, and wellness needs. To get started, consider how each recipe category in this cookbook can fit into different parts of your week.

Start by selecting three to four breakfasts that you can rotate throughout the week. These might include hormone-supporting smoothies, energy-boosting bowls, or quick oatmeal recipes packed with nuts and seeds. Preparing breakfasts in advance, like overnight oats or chia pudding, can save valuable time on busy mornings while ensuring that you're fueling up with foods that align with your health goals.

For lunches, choose recipes that can be prepared quickly or made in larger batches for leftovers. Salads with leafy greens, grilled protein, and fiber-rich toppings like chickpeas and quinoa are ideal, as they stay fresh and retain their nutrients when stored. Dinners can be a mix of light, nourishing meals that are easy to assemble after a long day. The cookbook's dinner recipes are crafted to be filling without being heavy, incorporating hormone-supporting ingredients like leafy greens, healthy fats, and lean proteins.

With these core meals selected, you'll have a foundation for balanced, nutrient-dense eating throughout the week. This approach reduces decision-making each day, streamlining your routine so that you can focus on enjoying your meals rather than planning them.

Tips for Meal Prep Success

Once your meal plan is in place, meal prep becomes a time-saving strategy to make each recipe come together effortlessly. Begin by setting aside a designated day or time each week to prepare the basics. Meal prep can be as simple as washing and chopping vegetables, cooking grains in batches, or portioning out snacks. Having pre-prepared ingredients on hand makes it much easier to assemble meals quickly, sticking to the 10-minute goal that defines this cookbook.

One useful approach is to "prep once, use twice." For instance, cook a batch of quinoa or brown rice at the beginning of the week, which can serve as a base for both lunches and dinners. Similarly, roasting a tray of vegetables or cooking proteins like grilled chicken or salmon in bulk gives you versatile ingredients that can be repurposed across multiple meals, from salads to wraps or bowls.

Another helpful tip is to portion snacks and breakfast items in advance. By pre-measuring nuts, seeds, and fruits, you can create grab-and-go options that keep you energized and prevent mid-morning hunger. Smoothie packs—pre-portioned bags with ingredients for smoothies—are also a great way to ensure a quick, nutrient-rich breakfast option that you can blend and enjoy in minutes.

Using the 10-Minute Recipes to Support Wellness Goals

This cookbook is structured to address specific wellness goals for women over 40, making it easy to tailor meal choices to support hormone health, energy levels, gut health, and weight management. By focusing on meals that align with your goals, you can build a meal plan that is not only time-efficient but also strategically beneficial for your health.

If hormone health is a primary concern, choose recipes rich in leafy greens, flaxseeds, cruciferous vegetables, and healthy fats. These foods help stabilize estrogen and progesterone levels, providing a natural way to manage hormonal changes. Adding dishes like the Kale & Sweet Potato Hormone Salad or Hormone-Balancing Avocado & Berry Smoothie into your routine can make a noticeable difference in your hormone health over time.

For energy support, prioritize recipes that include complex carbohydrates, protein, and healthy fats, as these macronutrients work together to stabilize blood sugar and prevent energy dips. The cookbook's Almond Butter & Banana Smoothie, Quinoa & Black Bean Salad, and Garlic Shrimp with Cauliflower Rice are ideal for supporting sustained energy throughout the day.

If weight management is your focus, aim for low-calorie, high-nutrient recipes that keep you feeling full without excessive calories. Balanced meals with fiber-rich vegetables, lean proteins, and healthy fats are effective for weight control, and you'll find plenty of options in the Sustainable Weight Loss chapter of this book. A typical day might include a Low-Calorie Berry & Almond Smoothie, Turkey Lettuce Wraps with Veggies for lunch, and a light Grilled Lemon Chicken with Steamed Broccoli for dinner.

Finally, if gut health is a key priority, select meals high in fiber and probiotic-rich ingredients. Foods like Greek yogurt, sauerkraut, leafy greens, and fibrous vegetables will nurture your gut microbiome, which in turn supports digestion, nutrient absorption, and immune health. Integrating recipes like the Probiotic Greek Yogurt & Berries Bowl and Kimchi & Cabbage Salad into your weekly plan will provide the diversity of nutrients and beneficial bacteria that support gut health.

Embracing Flexibility and Variety in Meal Planning

While a structured meal plan offers routine and simplicity, it's also important to embrace flexibility. The recipes in this cookbook can be adapted, switched around, and combined in creative ways. If you have a particularly busy day, opt for a quick smoothie or salad. On weekends, when you may have a little extra time, try a dinner recipe that includes more complex flavors or ingredients.

Maintaining variety is essential for both enjoyment and nutritional balance. Repeating recipes throughout the week can simplify your routine, but be sure to rotate ingredients or try new recipes occasionally to prevent taste fatigue and ensure that your diet remains rich in diverse nutrients.

When life gets busy, remember that even one nutrient-dense meal a day can have positive effects. By focusing on simplicity and sticking to the core principles of the 10-Minute Pelz Diet, you're making a commitment to your health that fits into your lifestyle, no matter how full your schedule may be.

Planning for Success with Realistic Goals

Setting realistic goals for meal planning is important, especially if you're new to preparing meals regularly or trying to introduce new eating habits. Instead of aiming for perfection, aim for consistency. Begin by planning a few breakfasts, lunches, and dinners each week, and gradually increase as you feel comfortable. This incremental approach prevents burnout and makes healthy eating feel manageable and sustainable.

Think of meal planning as an evolving process that adapts to your lifestyle. Your routine may change over time, and your meal plan can adjust accordingly. Use this cookbook as a guide, not a strict rulebook. It's here to make healthy eating enjoyable, accessible, and adaptable to your personal needs and preferences.

The Journey to Sustainable Health

The *10-Minute Pelz Diet Cookbook* is more than a collection of recipes; it's a pathway to sustainable health. By incorporating meal planning into your life, you're setting yourself up for a future where wellness is achievable, even on the busiest days. Each recipe and planning tip in this book is crafted to support you, empowering you to make small, positive changes that build lasting habits.

In the journey to optimal health, every meal counts. When meal planning feels overwhelming, remind yourself that these recipes are designed to simplify, not complicate, your routine. By focusing on nutrient-dense ingredients and easy preparation, you're creating a lifestyle that nourishes you from within, helping you feel vibrant, energized, and balanced as you navigate the demands of modern life.

Chapter 1: Quick & Easy Recipes for Hormone Balance

Achieving hormone balance is fundamental for women's health, especially as they navigate perimenopause, menopause, and the changes that come with midlife. Shifts in hormone levels can impact everything from energy and metabolism to mood and cognitive function. While these fluctuations are a natural part of aging, diet can significantly support hormonal stability, especially when nutrient-dense ingredients that promote balanced hormone function are integrated into daily meals. This chapter provides an array of breakfast, lunch, and dinner recipes designed to nourish the endocrine system and maintain equilibrium within the body. Each recipe focuses on key ingredients that stabilize blood sugar, support estrogen metabolism, and reduce inflammation, which are vital components in achieving and maintaining balanced hormones.

In addition to these hormone-supportive recipes, this chapter includes guidance on how fasting can aid women over 40. Dr. Mindy Pelz's approach to intermittent fasting offers a gentle yet effective way to manage weight, support metabolic health, and increase energy without creating undue stress on the body. These fasting tips are specifically tailored for women in midlife, providing insight into safely incorporating fasting for optimal health.

Fasting Tips for Hormone Balance

For women, fasting uniquely impacts hormone health. When approached thoughtfully, intermittent fasting improves insulin sensitivity, helps regulate cortisol, and boosts growth hormone levels—all of which support a balanced hormonal state. Here is an in-depth look at how fasting works to promote hormone health, especially for women experiencing midlife changes.

How Intermittent Fasting Can Help with Hormone Health

Intermittent fasting, often referred to as IF, is a pattern of cycling between eating and fasting periods. Unlike traditional diets that focus on what to eat, intermittent fasting emphasizes when to eat, allowing the body extended periods of rest between meals. For women over 40, intermittent fasting offers numerous benefits.

One of the primary ways fasting helps is by enhancing insulin sensitivity. As women age, the risk of insulin resistance increases, leading to potential weight gain, fatigue, and even a higher risk of type 2 diabetes. Fasting encourages the body to tap into stored glucose and later, stored fat, which promotes insulin sensitivity and keeps blood sugar levels stable. This stability can prevent energy crashes and reduce cravings, leading to more balanced energy throughout the day.

Fasting also promotes metabolic flexibility, meaning the body becomes more efficient at switching from burning glucose to burning fat for fuel. This ability is particularly beneficial for midlife women who may experience a slowing metabolism, making it easier to manage weight without strict calorie counting.

Growth hormone, another critical factor in women's health, plays a significant role in cell repair, metabolism, and muscle maintenance. With age, growth hormone levels naturally decline, but fasting helps stimulate growth hormone production, contributing to improved muscle tone, a healthy metabolism, and skin vitality—qualities that enhance women's overall well-being.

Fasting also reduces inflammation and supports cellular repair. The process, known as autophagy, involves the body's ability to clear out damaged cells, allowing for cellular renewal. Lower inflammation levels contribute to better overall health and longevity, which is especially valuable for women in midlife seeking vitality and resilience.

Finally, fasting aids in estrogen detoxification. The liver and gut work together to metabolize and eliminate excess estrogen, a process essential for hormone balance. Fasting gives the liver a much-needed break from continuous digestion, allowing it to focus on detoxification. By supporting these pathways, fasting promotes balanced estrogen levels and reduces symptoms often linked to excess estrogen, like bloating and mood swings.

Fasting Do's and Don'ts for Women Over 40

While fasting can offer significant benefits for hormone health, it's essential to approach it with sensitivity, as women's hormonal systems are particularly reactive to changes in routine. Starting with a gentle approach can help. Beginning with a 12-hour fasting window, such as fasting from 7 p.m. to 7 a.m., is an easy way to ease into fasting without intense hunger or fatigue. Over time, the fasting window can be extended to 14 or 16 hours, depending on how the body responds. It's important to proceed gradually and respect your body's cues.

Listening to the body is essential, as fasting should feel sustainable and supportive. If fasting causes fatigue, irritability, or intense hunger, adjusting the fasting window to a shorter period may help maintain a better balance. Every woman's body responds differently, so finding a rhythm that works is key to long-term success.

The meal that breaks your fast plays an equally important role in setting the tone for your day. Breaking the fast with nutrient-dense foods that contain a balance of protein, healthy fats, and fiber will stabilize blood sugar and prevent cravings later on. For instance, a smoothie made with almond milk, chia seeds, and berries or a yogurt bowl topped with nuts and seeds are both balanced and nourishing options that are easy on the digestive system and keep energy stable.

Hydration is another critical element in fasting. During fasting periods, drinking water or herbal teas ensures the body remains hydrated and can ease hunger pangs. Adding a bit of sea salt to water helps maintain electrolyte balance, which is beneficial for those new to fasting. Herbal teas or lemon water in the morning can provide a gentle, refreshing start and encourage digestive health.

Sleep and rest are equally essential when fasting, especially for women managing hormonal shifts. Rest supports the hormonal benefits of fasting by reducing cortisol, the body's primary stress hormone. Aiming for quality sleep of seven to nine hours each night enhances fasting's positive effects on hormone health, as sleep promotes cellular repair and balances cortisol levels.

One common mistake in fasting is fasting for extended periods (18 to 24 hours), which may not be beneficial for hormone health in women, particularly if practiced frequently. Long fasting periods can increase cortisol levels, adding stress to the body and potentially leading to hormonal imbalances. Instead, moderate fasting windows, such as 12 to 16 hours, often yield better results, offering the benefits of fasting without overtaxing the body.

Finally, it's essential to keep fasting flexible and adaptable to personal needs and lifestyle changes. Fasting should enhance well-being rather than feel like a restriction, allowing you to enjoy food and nourish your body without compromising balance. For women over 40, this balance between supportive fasting and sustainable eating is the cornerstone of achieving and maintaining hormone health.

Breakfast Recipes for Hormone Balance

Start your day with nutrient-dense breakfasts designed to support hormone health. Each recipe focuses on ingredients that stabilize blood sugar, promote hormone balance, and provide sustained energy, ensuring you feel nourished and balanced throughout the day.

Breakfast

1. Hormone-Balancing Avocado & Berry Smoothie

Description: A creamy, antioxidant-rich smoothie that combines hormone-supportive avocado with fiber-packed berries. Ideal for balancing blood sugar and providing steady energy.

Servings: 1 | **Prep time**: 5 minutes | **Cooking time**: 0 minutes

Ingredients:

➢ ½ avocado
➢ 1 cup mixed berries (strawberries, blueberries, raspberries)
➢ 1 cup almond milk (or other non-dairy milk)
➢ 1 tbsp chia seeds
➢ 1 tsp honey or maple syrup (optional)
➢ ½ cup ice cubes

Preparation Steps: Blend the avocado, berries, almond milk, chia seeds, honey, and ice until smooth. Adjust consistency as needed, then enjoy immediately for a nutritious start to your day.

Ratings: Calories: 290 kcal | Hormone Balance: 5/5 | Blood Sugar Stability: 5/5 | Sustained Energy: 4/5 | Anti-Inflammatory Support: 4/5 | Skin Health: 5/5

2. Chia & Flaxseed Power Oatmeal

Description: A hearty oatmeal, enhanced with chia and flaxseeds, rich in fiber and omega-3 fatty acids. This breakfast supports hormone balance and digestive health, keeping you full and energized.

Servings: 1 | **Prep time**: 5 minutes | **Cooking time**: 5 minutes

Ingredients:

➢ ½ cup rolled oats
➢ 1 tbsp chia seeds
➢ 1 tbsp ground flaxseeds
➢ 1 cup almond milk (or milk of choice)
➢ ½ tsp cinnamon
➢ 1 tsp honey or maple syrup (optional)

Preparation Steps: In a small saucepan, combine the oats, chia seeds, flaxseeds, and almond milk. Simmer over medium heat, stirring occasionally until the oats are soft and creamy, about 5 minutes. Add cinnamon and sweetener, stir, and serve warm.

Ratings: Calories: 320 kcal | Hormone Balance: 5/5 | Digestive Health: 5/5 | Blood Sugar Stability: 5/5 | Omega-3 Support: 5/5 | Long-Lasting Fullness: 5/5

3. Apple & Cinnamon Quinoa Porridge

Description: A comforting quinoa porridge with apples and cinnamon, providing protein, fiber, and hormone-supportive nutrients, perfect for a balanced and warming breakfast.

Servings: 2 | **Prep time**: 5 minutes | **Cooking time**: 15 minutes

Ingredients:

➢ 1 cup cooked quinoa
➢ ½ apple, diced
➢ 1 cup almond milk (or other milk of choice)
➢ ½ tsp cinnamon
➢ 1 tbsp maple syrup or honey
➢ 1 tbsp chopped walnuts (optional)

Preparation Steps: In a saucepan, combine cooked quinoa, almond milk, diced apple, and cinnamon. Bring to a simmer over medium heat, stirring frequently until the apple softens and the porridge thickens, about 10–15 minutes.

Stir in maple syrup and top with walnuts before serving.

Ratings: Calories: 350 kcal | Hormone Balance: 5/5 | Energy Boost: 4/5 | Protein Support: 5/5 | Blood Sugar Stability: 4/5 | Antioxidant Support: 4/5

4. Hormone-Supporting Sweet Potato Hash

Description: A savory breakfast rich in complex carbs and antioxidants, this sweet potato hash supports blood sugar balance and provides steady energy throughout the morning.

Servings: 2 | Prep time: 5 minutes | Cooking time: 10 minutes

Ingredients:

➢ 1 medium sweet potato, peeled and diced
➢ 1 bell pepper, diced
➢ ½ small onion, diced
➢ 1 tbsp olive oil
➢ Salt and pepper to taste
➢ 1 tsp smoked paprika
➢ Fresh parsley for garnish (optional)

Preparation Steps: Heat olive oil in a skillet over medium heat. Add sweet potato, bell pepper, and onion, seasoning with salt, pepper, and smoked paprika. Sauté for about 10 minutes, stirring occasionally, until sweet potato is tender and vegetables are golden. Sprinkle with fresh parsley if desired.

Ratings: Calories: 220 kcal | Blood Sugar Stability: 5/5 | Hormone Support: 5/5 |

Antioxidant Richness: 4/5 | Fiber Support: 5/5 | Long-Lasting Fullness: 4/5

5. Almond & Seed Breakfast Bowl

Description: A nourishing breakfast bowl packed with healthy fats and fiber, promoting hormone balance and keeping you satisfied all morning.

Servings: 1 | Prep time: 5 minutes | Cooking time: 0 minutes

Ingredients:

➢ 1 cup unsweetened Greek yogurt or coconut yogurt
➢ 1 tbsp almond butter
➢ 1 tbsp chia seeds
➢ 1 tbsp pumpkin seeds
➢ 1 tbsp sliced almonds
➢ 1 tsp honey or maple syrup (optional)
➢ Fresh berries for topping

Preparation Steps: In a bowl, combine the yogurt with almond butter and mix until smooth. Top with chia seeds, pumpkin seeds, and sliced almonds, adding honey for sweetness if desired. Add fresh berries to enhance flavor and nutrients, then enjoy.

Ratings: Calories: 280 kcal | Hormone Balance: 5/5 | Blood Sugar Stability: 5/5 | Digestive Health: 4/5 | Healthy Fats: 5/5 | Satiety Factor: 5/5

6. Green Tea & Almond Smoothie

Description: A refreshing smoothie that combines green tea's antioxidant power with almond milk and healthy fats for a light, energizing breakfast that supports hormone health.

Servings: 1 | **Prep time**: 5 minutes | **Cooking time**: 0 minutes

Ingredients:

➢ 1 cup brewed and cooled green tea
➢ 1 cup almond milk
➢ ½ avocado
➢ 1 tbsp chia seeds
➢ 1 tsp honey or maple syrup (optional)

Preparation Steps: Blend green tea, almond milk, avocado, chia seeds, and honey until smooth. Serve immediately for a refreshing, hormone-supportive start to the day.

Ratings: Calories: 210 kcal | Hormone Support: 4/5 | Antioxidant Power: 5/5 | Energy Boost: 4/5 | Healthy Fats: 5/5 | Blood Sugar Stability: 5/5

7. Berry & Protein Yogurt Parfait

Description: This parfait layers Greek yogurt with berries and seeds, delivering protein and antioxidants to support hormone balance and energy.

Servings: 1 | **Prep time**: 5 minutes | **Cooking time**: 0 minutes

Ingredients:

➢ 1 cup Greek yogurt (or dairy-free yogurt)
➢ ½ cup mixed berries
➢ 1 tbsp chia seeds
➢ 1 tbsp pumpkin seeds
➢ 1 tsp honey (optional)

Preparation Steps: In a bowl or glass, layer the Greek yogurt with mixed berries. Top with chia seeds, pumpkin seeds, and a drizzle of honey if desired. Enjoy as a protein-rich, hormone-supportive breakfast.

Ratings: Calories: 250 kcal | Protein Boost: 5/5 | Hormone Balance: 5/5 | Digestive Health: 4/5 | Antioxidant Support: 5/5 | Blood Sugar Stability: 5/5

8. Golden Milk Overnight Oats

Description: A warm and comforting blend of turmeric and cinnamon in this overnight oats recipe offers anti-inflammatory benefits to support hormone health and balance.

Servings: 1 | **Prep time**: 5 minutes | **Cooking time**: 0 minutes

Ingredients:

➢ ½ cup rolled oats
➢ 1 cup almond milk (or milk of choice)
➢ ½ tsp turmeric powder
➢ ¼ tsp cinnamon
➢ 1 tbsp chia seeds
➢ 1 tsp honey or maple syrup (optional)
➢ Pinch of black pepper

Preparation Steps: In a mason jar or bowl, combine oats, almond milk, turmeric, cinnamon, chia seeds, honey, and a pinch of black pepper. Stir well to incorporate all ingredients, cover, and refrigerate overnight. In the morning, give it a quick stir and enjoy cold or warmed up.

Ratings: Calories: 300 kcal | Anti-Inflammatory Support: 5/5 | Hormone Balance: 4/5 | Digestive Health: 5/5 | Blood Sugar Stability: 4/5 | Energy Boost: 4/5

9. Pumpkin Seed & Coconut Granola

Description: This crunchy granola with pumpkin seeds and coconut provides healthy fats, fiber, and zinc—nutrients that support hormone health and overall wellness.

Servings: 4 | **Prep time**: 5 minutes | **Cooking time**: 15 minutes

Ingredients:

➤ 1 cup rolled oats
➤ ¼ cup pumpkin seeds
➤ ¼ cup shredded coconut
➤ 1 tbsp chia seeds
➤ 1 tbsp coconut oil, melted
➤ 1 tbsp honey or maple syrup

Preparation Steps: Preheat oven to 325°F (160°C). In a large bowl, mix oats, pumpkin seeds, shredded coconut, and chia seeds. Drizzle with melted coconut oil and honey, stirring to coat. Spread the mixture evenly on a baking sheet and bake for 10-15 minutes, stirring halfway through, until golden brown. Allow to cool and store in an airtight container.

Ratings: Calories: 220 kcal | Healthy Fats: 5/5 | Hormone Support: 4/5 | Digestive Health: 4/5 | Satiety Factor: 4/5 | Blood Sugar Stability: 4/5

10. Hormone-Friendly Egg & Veggie Scramble

Description: A quick, savory scramble packed with protein, fiber, and colorful veggies to support hormone balance and keep you energized.

Servings: 1 | **Prep time**: 5 minutes | **Cooking time**: 5 minutes

Ingredients:

➤ 2 large eggs
➤ ¼ cup diced bell peppers
➤ ¼ cup spinach leaves
➤ 1 tbsp diced onion
➤ 1 tsp olive oil
➤ Salt and pepper to taste

Preparation Steps: Heat olive oil in a skillet over medium heat. Add the bell peppers, spinach, and onion, sautéing until tender. In a small bowl, whisk the eggs, then pour them into the skillet with the veggies. Cook, stirring gently, until eggs are scrambled to your liking. Season with salt and pepper and serve immediately.

Ratings: Calories: 200 kcal | Protein Support: 5/5 | Hormone Balance: 5/5 | Digestive Health: 4/5 | Energy Boost: 5/5 | Blood Sugar Stability: 4/5

11. Flaxseed & Apple Smoothie Bowl

Description: This smoothie bowl blends apple, flaxseed, and greens for a refreshing and fiber-rich breakfast that supports hormone health and digestion.

Servings: 1 | **Prep time**: 5 minutes | **Cooking time**: 0 minutes

Ingredients:

➤ 1 apple, chopped
➤ 1 cup spinach leaves
➤ 1 cup almond milk
➤ 1 tbsp ground flaxseed
➤ 1 tsp honey or maple syrup (optional)
➤ Toppings: sliced almonds, chia seeds, fresh berries

Preparation Steps: Blend the apple, spinach, almond milk, and flaxseed until smooth. Pour into a bowl and top with sliced almonds, chia seeds, and fresh berries for added nutrients and crunch.

Ratings: Calories: 250 kcal | Fiber Support: 5/5 | Hormone Balance: 4/5 | Antioxidant Boost: 4/5 | Digestive Health: 5/5 | Blood Sugar Stability: 4/5

12. Spiced Walnut & Banana Oatmeal

Description: A comforting bowl of oatmeal with warming spices, banana, and walnuts for a breakfast rich in healthy fats, fiber, and hormone-supportive nutrients.

Servings: 1 | **Prep time**: 5 minutes | **Cooking time**: 5 minutes

Ingredients:

➤ ½ cup rolled oats
➤ 1 cup almond milk (or other milk of choice)
➤ ½ banana, sliced
➤ 1 tbsp chopped walnuts

➤ ¼ tsp cinnamon
➤ 1 tsp honey or maple syrup (optional)

Preparation Steps: In a small saucepan, combine oats and almond milk, bringing to a simmer over medium heat. Cook for about 5 minutes, stirring frequently until oats are soft and creamy. Add cinnamon and sliced banana, stirring to incorporate. Top with walnuts and a drizzle of honey if desired.

Ratings: Calories: 300 kcal | Hormone Balance: 5/5 | Heart Health: 4/5 | Digestive Health: 5/5 | Energy Boost: 4/5 | Satiety Factor: 4/5

Lunch

13. Kale & Sweet Potato Hormone Salad

Description: A nutrient-dense salad combining kale and sweet potatoes, providing fiber, antioxidants, and complex carbs to support hormone balance and sustained energy.

Servings: 2 | **Prep time**: 10 minutes | **Cooking time**: 15 minutes

Ingredients:

➤ 2 cups kale, chopped
➤ 1 medium sweet potato, diced and roasted
➤ ¼ cup pumpkin seeds
➤ ¼ cup diced red bell pepper
➤ 1 tbsp olive oil
➤ 1 tbsp lemon juice
➤ Salt and pepper to taste

Preparation Steps: Roast the sweet potato in a preheated oven at 400°F (200°C) for 15 minutes or until tender. Meanwhile, massage kale with olive oil and lemon juice in a large bowl until tender. Add the roasted sweet potato, pumpkin seeds, and bell pepper, tossing everything together. Season with salt and pepper and serve.

Ratings: Calories: 280 kcal | Hormone Balance: 5/5 | Fiber Support: 5/5 | Antioxidant Power: 4/5 | Digestive Health: 5/5 | Blood Sugar Stability: 4/5

14. Spinach Wrap with Hummus & Sprouts

Description: A light and refreshing spinach wrap filled with hummus, sprouts, and veggies, delivering fiber and plant-based protein for balanced hormones and sustained energy.

Servings: 1 | **Prep time**: 5 minutes | **Cooking time**: 0 minutes

Ingredients:

➢ 1 large spinach or whole-grain wrap
➢ 2 tbsp hummus
➢ ½ cup fresh spinach leaves
➢ ¼ cup alfalfa or broccoli sprouts
➢ ¼ cup shredded carrots
➢ ¼ cucumber, sliced

Preparation Steps: Spread hummus evenly over the wrap. Layer with spinach, sprouts, shredded carrots, and cucumber slices. Roll tightly, slice in half, and enjoy a fresh and nutrient-packed lunch.

Ratings: Calories: 230 kcal | Hormone Balance: 4/5 | Fiber Support: 5/5 | Plant-Based Protein: 4/5 | Digestive Health: 5/5 | Energy Boost: 4/5

15. Lentil & Avocado Buddha Bowl

Description: A balanced Buddha bowl packed with lentils, avocado, and colorful veggies, providing protein, fiber, and healthy fats for hormone support and blood sugar stability.

Servings: 2 | **Prep time**: 10 minutes | **Cooking time**: 20 minutes

Ingredients:

➢ 1 cup cooked lentils
➢ ½ avocado, sliced
➢ 1 cup mixed greens
➢ ¼ cup shredded carrots
➢ ¼ cup cucumber, diced
➢ 1 tbsp tahini
➢ 1 tbsp lemon juice
➢ Salt and pepper to taste

Preparation Steps: Arrange the lentils, avocado, mixed greens, carrots, and cucumber in a bowl. Drizzle with tahini and lemon juice, then season with salt and pepper. Serve immediately for a satisfying, hormone-friendly meal.

Ratings: Calories: 320 kcal | Hormone Balance: 5/5 | Fiber Support: 5/5 | Healthy Fats: 4/5 | Blood Sugar Stability: 5/5 | Satiety Factor: 5/5

16. Roasted Beet & Walnut Salad

Description: A vibrant salad featuring roasted beets and walnuts, offering antioxidants, fiber, and omega-3s to support hormone health and overall wellness.

Servings: 2 | **Prep time**: 10 minutes | **Cooking time**: 30 minutes

Ingredients:

➤ 2 medium beets, roasted and sliced
➤ 4 cups mixed greens
➤ ¼ cup walnuts, chopped
➤ 1 tbsp balsamic vinegar
➤ 1 tbsp olive oil
➤ Salt and pepper to taste

Preparation Steps: Roast the beets in a preheated oven at 400°F (200°C) for 30 minutes, until tender. In a large bowl, combine mixed greens, sliced beets, and walnuts. Drizzle with balsamic vinegar and olive oil, then season with salt and pepper before serving.

Ratings: Calories: 240 kcal | Hormone Balance: 4/5 | Antioxidant Power: 5/5 | Omega-3 Support: 4/5 | Digestive Health: 4/5 | Blood Sugar Stability: 4/5

17. Mediterranean Chickpea & Feta Salad

Description: A Mediterranean-inspired salad with chickpeas, feta, and fresh vegetables, providing protein, fiber, and antioxidants for hormone balance and energy.

Servings: 2 | **Prep time**: 10 minutes | **Cooking time**: 0 minutes

Ingredients:

➤ 1 cup canned chickpeas, rinsed and drained
➤ ½ cup diced cucumber
➤ ½ cup cherry tomatoes, halved
➤ ¼ cup crumbled feta cheese
➤ 2 tbsp fresh parsley, chopped
➤ 1 tbsp olive oil
➤ 1 tbsp lemon juice
➤ Salt and pepper to taste

Preparation Steps: In a large bowl, combine chickpeas, cucumber, cherry tomatoes, feta, and parsley. Drizzle with olive oil and lemon juice, season with salt and pepper, and toss to combine. Serve immediately.

Ratings: Calories: 290 kcal | Hormone Balance: 4/5 | Protein Support: 4/5 | Fiber Support: 5/5 | Blood Sugar Stability: 5/5 | Antioxidant Power: 4/5

18. Hormone-Balancing Quinoa & Kale Bowl

Description: This bowl combines quinoa, kale, and vibrant veggies, packed with fiber and nutrients to support hormone health and sustained energy.

Servings: 2 | **Prep time**: 10 minutes | **Cooking time**: 15 minutes

Ingredients:

➤ 1 cup cooked quinoa
➤ 2 cups kale, chopped
➤ ½ cup shredded carrots
➤ ¼ cup pumpkin seeds
➤ 1 tbsp olive oil

> ➢ 1 tbsp apple cider vinegar
> ➢ Salt and pepper to taste

Preparation Steps: In a bowl, combine the cooked quinoa, kale, carrots, and pumpkin seeds. Drizzle with olive oil and apple cider vinegar, season with salt and pepper, and toss to combine. Serve as a nutrient-dense meal for hormone balance.

Ratings: Calories: 310 kcal | Hormone Balance: 5/5 | Fiber Support: 5/5 | Digestive Health: 5/5 | Blood Sugar Stability: 5/5 | Antioxidant Power: 4/5

19. Collard Green Wraps with Tofu & Mixed Greens

Description: Collard greens serve as a nutritious wrap filled with tofu and veggies, providing plant-based protein, fiber, and antioxidants for hormone support.

Servings: 1 | **Prep time**: 10 minutes | **Cooking time**: 0 minutes

Ingredients:

> ➢ 2 large collard green leaves
> ➢ ½ cup tofu, cubed
> ➢ ¼ cup shredded carrots
> ➢ ¼ cup cucumber, sliced
> ➢ ½ avocado, sliced
> ➢ 1 tbsp tahini

Preparation Steps: Lay the collard greens flat, then add tofu, carrots, cucumber, and avocado down the center. Drizzle with tahini, roll tightly, and slice in half to serve.

Ratings: Calories: 250 kcal | Hormone Balance: 5/5 | Plant-Based Protein: 4/5 | Fiber Support: 5/5 | Antioxidant Support: 4/5 | Blood Sugar Stability: 4/5

20. Citrus Chicken & Spinach Salad

Description: A refreshing salad with citrus-marinated chicken and spinach, providing lean protein, vitamins, and antioxidants for hormone health and energy.

Servings: 2 | **Prep time**: 10 minutes | **Cooking time**: 15 minutes

Ingredients:

> ➢ 1 chicken breast, cooked and sliced
> ➢ 3 cups spinach leaves
> ➢ ½ orange, segmented
> ➢ 1 tbsp olive oil
> ➢ 1 tbsp lemon juice
> ➢ Salt and pepper to taste

Preparation Steps: Arrange spinach in a bowl, then top with sliced chicken and orange segments. Drizzle with olive oil and lemon juice, season with salt and pepper, and toss gently before serving.

Ratings: Calories: 290 kcal | Protein Support: 5/5 | Hormone Balance: 4/5 | Antioxidant Power: 4/5 | Energy Boost: 5/5 | Blood Sugar Stability: 5/5

21. Roasted Squash & Spinach Salad

Description: A warm salad featuring roasted squash and fresh spinach, offering complex carbs, fiber, and nutrients that support hormone balance.

Servings: 2 | **Prep time**: 10 minutes | **Cooking time**: 20 minutes

Ingredients:

➢ 1 cup cubed butternut squash, roasted
➢ 2 cups spinach leaves
➢ ¼ cup pomegranate seeds
➢ 1 tbsp balsamic vinegar
➢ 1 tbsp olive oil

Preparation Steps: Roast the butternut squash at 400°F (200°C) for 20 minutes. Arrange spinach in a bowl, top with squash and pomegranate seeds, and drizzle with balsamic vinegar and olive oil.

Ratings: Calories: 260 kcal | Hormone Balance: 4/5 | Antioxidant Power: 5/5 | Digestive Health: 4/5 | Blood Sugar Stability: 4/5 | Energy Boost: 4/5

22. Hormone-Boosting Veggie Stuffed Sweet Potatoes

Description: Stuffed sweet potatoes with a mix of hormone-supportive veggies provide fiber, complex carbs, and essential vitamins for a balanced lunch.

Servings: 2 | **Prep time**: 5 minutes | **Cooking time**: 30 minutes

Ingredients:

➢ 2 medium sweet potatoes, baked
➢ ¼ cup chickpeas
➢ ¼ cup diced bell pepper
➢ ¼ cup spinach leaves
➢ 1 tbsp tahini

Preparation Steps: Slice baked sweet potatoes and fill with chickpeas, bell pepper, and spinach. Drizzle with tahini and serve.

Ratings: Calories: 300 kcal | Fiber Support: 5/5 | Hormone Balance: 5/5 | Digestive Health: 4/5 | Blood Sugar Stability: 5/5 | Antioxidant Power: 4/5

23. Grilled Eggplant & Red Pepper Salad

Description: A smoky, flavorful salad with grilled eggplant and red pepper, rich in fiber and antioxidants to support hormone balance and digestion.

Servings: 2 | **Prep time**: 10 minutes | **Cooking time**: 15 minutes

Ingredients:

➢ 1 medium eggplant, sliced and grilled
➢ 1 red bell pepper, sliced and grilled
➢ 2 cups arugula
➢ 1 tbsp olive oil
➢ Salt and pepper to taste

Preparation Steps: Grill the eggplant and red pepper slices until tender. Combine with arugula, drizzle with olive oil, and season with salt and pepper.

Ratings: Calories: 220 kcal | Antioxidant Power: 5/5 | Hormone Balance: 4/5 | Digestive Health: 5/5 | Blood Sugar Stability: 4/5 | Satiety Factor: 4/5

24. Carrot & Ginger Hormone-Boosting Soup

Description: A warming, hormone-supportive soup made with carrots and ginger, which provides anti-inflammatory and antioxidant benefits.

Servings: 2 | **Prep time**: 10 minutes | **Cooking time**: 15 minutes

Ingredients:

➢ 4 carrots, chopped
➢ 1 tbsp grated ginger
➢ 2 cups vegetable broth
➢ 1 tbsp olive oil

Preparation Steps: Sauté carrots and ginger in olive oil until tender. Add vegetable broth, simmering until carrots are soft, then blend until smooth.

Ratings: Calories: 180 kcal | Hormone Balance: 5/5 | Anti-Inflammatory Support: 5/5 | Digestive Health: 4/5 | Energy Boost: 4/5 | Blood Sugar Stability: 4/5

Dinner

25. Wild-Caught Salmon with Roasted Asparagus

Description: A light and flavorful dinner with omega-3-rich salmon and fiber-packed asparagus, perfect for supporting hormone health, skin health, and anti-inflammatory benefits.

Servings: 2 | **Prep time**: 5 minutes | **Cooking time**: 15 minutes

Ingredients:

➢ 2 wild-caught salmon fillets
➢ 1 bunch asparagus, trimmed

➢ 1 tbsp olive oil
➢ Salt and pepper to taste
➢ 1 lemon, sliced

Preparation Steps: Preheat the oven to 400°F (200°C). Place salmon and asparagus on a baking sheet, drizzle with olive oil, and season with salt and pepper. Top with lemon slices and bake for 12-15 minutes or until salmon flakes easily with a fork. Serve warm.

Ratings: Calories: 320 kcal | Hormone Balance: 5/5 | Omega-3 Support: 5/5 | Anti-Inflammatory Properties: 5/5 | Skin Health: 5/5 | Blood Sugar Stability: 4/5

26. Chickpea Stew with Spinach & Turmeric

Description: A hearty, anti-inflammatory chickpea stew loaded with spinach and turmeric, supporting hormone balance, immune health, and digestion.

Servings: 2 | **Prep time**: 10 minutes | **Cooking time**: 20 minutes

Ingredients:

➢ 1 cup canned chickpeas, rinsed and drained
➢ 2 cups spinach
➢ 1 tbsp olive oil
➢ 1 tsp turmeric powder
➢ 2 cups vegetable broth
➢ Salt and pepper to taste

Preparation Steps: Heat olive oil in a pot over medium heat, add turmeric, and cook until fragrant. Add chickpeas, spinach, and vegetable broth, bringing to a simmer for

15-20 minutes. Season with salt and pepper before serving.

Ratings: Calories: 260 kcal | Hormone Balance: 5/5 | Anti-Inflammatory Support: 5/5 | Immune Health: 4/5 | Digestive Health: 4/5 | Blood Sugar Stability: 5/5

27. Baked Turmeric Cauliflower & Sweet Potatoes

Description: A warming, nutrient-dense side with turmeric-spiced cauliflower and sweet potatoes, delivering anti-inflammatory benefits and hormone-supporting nutrients.

Servings: 2 | **Prep time**: 5 minutes | **Cooking time**: 25 minutes

Ingredients:

➢ 1 cup cauliflower florets
➢ 1 medium sweet potato, cubed
➢ 1 tbsp olive oil
➢ 1 tsp turmeric powder
➢ Salt and pepper to taste

Preparation Steps: Preheat oven to 400°F (200°C). Toss cauliflower and sweet potato with olive oil and turmeric, spread on a baking sheet, and roast for 25 minutes or until tender. Season with salt and pepper before serving.

Ratings: Calories: 220 kcal | Anti-Inflammatory Support: 5/5 | Hormone Balance: 4/5 | Digestive Health: 4/5 | Blood Sugar Stability: 4/5 | Antioxidant Power: 5/5

28. Black Bean & Sweet Potato Enchiladas

Description: Delicious enchiladas filled with black beans and sweet potatoes, providing fiber, protein, and nutrients that support hormone health and satiety.

Servings: 4 | **Prep time**: 10 minutes | **Cooking time**: 20 minutes

Ingredients:

➢ 1 cup black beans, rinsed and drained
➢ 1 medium sweet potato, diced and roasted
➢ 4 whole-grain tortillas
➢ 1 cup enchilada sauce
➢ ½ cup shredded cheese (optional)

Preparation Steps: Preheat oven to 375°F (190°C). In a bowl, combine black beans and roasted sweet potatoes. Fill tortillas with the mixture, roll, and place in a baking dish. Pour enchilada sauce over tortillas and sprinkle with cheese if desired. Bake for 20 minutes and serve warm.

Ratings: Calories: 320 kcal | Fiber Support: 5/5 | Hormone Balance: 4/5 | Satiety Factor: 5/5 | Digestive Health: 4/5 | Blood Sugar Stability: 4/5

29. Grilled Cod with Brussels Sprouts & Carrots

Description: A light, omega-3-rich dinner of grilled cod served with fiber-rich Brussels sprouts and carrots, supporting hormone balance and anti-inflammatory health.

Servings: 2 | **Prep time**: 10 minutes | **Cooking time**: 15 minutes

Ingredients:

➢ 2 cod fillets
➢ 1 cup Brussels sprouts, halved
➢ 1 cup carrots, sliced
➢ 1 tbsp olive oil
➢ Salt and pepper to taste

Preparation Steps: Preheat grill to medium-high. Drizzle cod, Brussels sprouts, and carrots with olive oil, season with salt and pepper, and grill until cod is cooked through and vegetables are tender, about 15 minutes. Serve immediately.

Ratings: Calories: 290 kcal | Omega-3 Support: 4/5 | Hormone Balance: 5/5 | Digestive Health: 4/5 | Anti-Inflammatory Support: 5/5 | Blood Sugar Stability: 4/5

30. Hormone-Supporting Mushroom & Spinach Stir Fry

Description: This quick stir fry features mushrooms and spinach, both packed with nutrients that support hormone balance, bone health, and overall wellness.

Servings: 2 | **Prep time**: 5 minutes | **Cooking time**: 10 minutes

Ingredients:

➢ 2 cups mushrooms, sliced
➢ 2 cups spinach
➢ 1 tbsp olive oil
➢ 1 tsp garlic, minced
➢ Salt and pepper to taste

Preparation Steps: Heat olive oil in a skillet over medium heat. Add garlic and mushrooms, cooking until mushrooms soften. Add spinach, cooking until wilted, and season with salt and pepper. Serve hot as a main or side.

Ratings: Calories: 180 kcal | Hormone Balance: 5/5 | Bone Health: 4/5 | Anti-Inflammatory Support: 4/5 | Digestive Health: 4/5 | Satiety Factor: 4/5

31. Ginger Chicken with Roasted Vegetables

Description: A warming ginger-spiced chicken served with roasted vegetables for an anti-inflammatory, hormone-supporting meal rich in protein and fiber.

Servings: 2 | **Prep time**: 10 minutes | **Cooking time**: 25 minutes

Ingredients:

➢ 1 chicken breast, sliced
➢ 1 tbsp grated ginger
➢ 1 cup carrots, sliced
➢ 1 cup broccoli florets
➢ 1 tbsp olive oil

Preparation Steps: Preheat oven to 400°F (200°C). Toss chicken with ginger, and coat vegetables in olive oil. Spread everything on a baking sheet, roasting for 20-25 minutes until chicken is cooked and vegetables are tender.

Ratings: Calories: 300 kcal | Anti-Inflammatory Support: 5/5 | Protein Support: 5/5 | Hormone Balance: 4/5 |

Digestive Health: 4/5 | Blood Sugar Stability: 4/5

32. Roasted Squash & Carrot Medley

Description: A colorful, roasted squash and carrot dish with fiber and antioxidants, perfect for supporting hormone health, immune function, and digestion.

Servings: 2 | **Prep time**: 5 minutes | **Cooking time**: 25 minutes

Ingredients:

➤ 1 cup cubed butternut squash
➤ 1 cup sliced carrots
➤ 1 tbsp olive oil
➤ Salt and pepper to taste

Preparation Steps: Preheat oven to 400°F (200°C). Toss squash and carrots in olive oil, season with salt and pepper, and roast on a baking sheet for 25 minutes or until tender.

Ratings: Calories: 220 kcal | Hormone Balance: 4/5 | Antioxidant Support: 5/5 | Digestive Health: 4/5 | Immune Health: 4/5 | Blood Sugar Stability: 4/5

33. Basil Pesto Zoodles with Shrimp

Description: A light, gluten-free dish with zoodles and shrimp in basil pesto, providing protein, healthy fats, and hormone-supportive nutrients.

Servings: 2 | **Prep time**: 10 minutes | **Cooking time**: 5 minutes

Ingredients:

➤ 2 cups zucchini noodles (zoodles)
➤ 1 cup shrimp, peeled and deveined
➤ 2 tbsp basil pesto
➤ 1 tbsp olive oil

Preparation Steps: Heat olive oil in a skillet, add shrimp, and cook until pink. Toss zoodles with pesto, then add cooked shrimp and serve.

Ratings: Calories: 280 kcal | Protein Support: 5/5 | Hormone Balance: 4/5 | Healthy Fats: 4/5 | Digestive Health: 4/5 | Blood Sugar Stability: 4/5

34. Quinoa Stuffed Bell Peppers

Description: Colorful bell peppers stuffed with quinoa, vegetables, and herbs, providing fiber, protein, and nutrients to support hormone health and satiety.

Servings: 2 | **Prep time**: 10 minutes | **Cooking time**: 20 minutes

Ingredients:

➤ 2 bell peppers, halved and seeded
➤ 1 cup cooked quinoa
➤ ¼ cup diced tomatoes
➤ 1 tbsp chopped parsley
➤ Salt and pepper to taste

Preparation Steps: Preheat oven to 375°F (190°C). Stuff peppers with quinoa, tomatoes, and parsley. Place in a baking dish and bake for 20 minutes until peppers are tender.

Ratings: Calories: 300 kcal | Fiber Support: 5/5 | Hormone Balance: 4/5 | Satiety Factor: 5/5 | Digestive Health: 4/5 | Blood Sugar Stability: 4/5

35. Spicy Lentil & Veggie Curry

Description: A warming, spicy lentil curry packed with veggies and spices, providing fiber, plant-based protein, and anti-inflammatory benefits for hormone health.

Servings: 2 | **Prep time**: 10 minutes | **Cooking time**: 25 minutes

Ingredients:

➤ 1 cup lentils, cooked
➤ 1 cup mixed vegetables (carrots, peas, bell pepper)
➤ 1 cup coconut milk
➤ 1 tbsp curry powder

Preparation Steps: In a pot, combine lentils, vegetables, coconut milk, and curry powder. Simmer for 20-25 minutes until thickened, and serve warm.

Ratings: Calories: 320 kcal | Hormone Balance: 4/5 | Fiber Support: 5/5 | Anti-Inflammatory Support: 5/5 | Digestive Health: 4/5 | Blood Sugar Stability: 4/5

36. Herb-Marinated Grilled Tofu

Description: Grilled tofu marinated in fresh herbs and spices, offering plant-based protein, fiber, and hormone-supportive nutrients.

Servings: 2 | **Prep time**: 15 minutes | **Cooking time**: 10 minutes

Ingredients:

➤ 1 cup tofu, cubed
➤ 1 tbsp olive oil
➤ 1 tbsp fresh herbs (basil, thyme, or rosemary)
➤ Salt and pepper to taste

Preparation Steps: Marinate tofu in olive oil and herbs for 10 minutes. Grill until golden and crisp, seasoning with salt and pepper. Serve warm.

Ratings: Calories: 250 kcal | Plant-Based Protein: 5/5 | Hormone Balance: 4/5 | Fiber Support: 4/5 | Digestive Health: 4/5 | Blood Sugar Stability: 4/5

Chapter 2: Recipes for Lasting Energy

Navigating a busy day requires more than just a quick boost of energy; it's about maintaining steady stamina and focus without experiencing those dreaded mid-afternoon slumps. This chapter offers a selection of recipes designed to promote lasting energy through balanced macronutrients and nutrient-dense ingredients. These meals provide the right combination of proteins, healthy fats, and complex carbohydrates to stabilize blood sugar, prevent energy dips, and fuel your body throughout the day. Whether you're juggling work, family, or personal projects, these recipes are crafted to help you stay energized and focused.

In addition to these energy-sustaining meals, this chapter includes practical fasting tips specifically tailored for maintaining high energy levels. Combining fasting with energy-focused meals can maximize your body's natural rhythms, supporting metabolic health and mental clarity without feeling drained. These tips will guide you in selecting the best fasting schedules for sustained energy, ensuring that you harness the benefits of intermittent fasting while keeping your vitality intact.

Energy-Boosting Fasting Tips

Intermittent fasting, when thoughtfully practiced, can be a powerful tool for managing energy. Rather than focusing on restricting calories, fasting optimizes when you eat, helping your body naturally regulate its energy cycles. With an approach focused on steady, accessible energy, these tips provide a roadmap for combining fasting with energy-sustaining meals, ensuring that you feel refreshed, alert, and ready for the day.

Combining Fasting with Energy-Focused Meals

Integrating intermittent fasting with meals designed for energy support involves selecting foods that nourish the body in ways that complement the fasting process. Breaking your fast with balanced macronutrients—protein, healthy fats, and complex carbohydrates—supports the body's return to an active metabolism while keeping energy stable. This combination fuels you without the sharp blood sugar spikes and subsequent crashes that can occur after a heavy meal. Starting your eating window with a balanced, energy-focused meal, like a smoothie rich in protein and healthy fats or a salad topped with lean proteins and fiber-dense vegetables, keeps you feeling full without weighing you down.

Another essential aspect of combining fasting with energy-boosting meals is timing. Plan your first meal so it aligns with your body's natural circadian rhythm, generally between late morning and early afternoon, depending on your fasting schedule. This approach maximizes your energy production at times when your body is naturally inclined to be more alert, making it easier to maintain focus and productivity throughout the day. By focusing on nutrient-dense meals at the start of your eating window, you avoid the mid-day slump and feel more energized well into the evening.

Best Fasting Schedules for Energy Maintenance

Selecting a fasting schedule that aligns with your energy needs can make a significant difference in how you feel throughout the day. For those new to fasting or those seeking a balanced routine, a 12:12 fasting schedule, where you fast for 12 hours and eat within a 12-hour window, provides gentle benefits without requiring a significant adjustment to your usual routine. This schedule can help maintain consistent energy by allowing your body time to rest and repair overnight while providing flexibility for an early breakfast and a dinner before your fasting window begins.

For those who have experience with fasting, a 14:10 or 16:8 schedule can support energy maintenance effectively. With a 14-hour fast followed by a 10-hour eating window, or a 16-hour fast followed by an 8-hour eating window, you gain additional metabolic benefits, such as improved insulin sensitivity and a greater reliance on stored fat for energy. These schedules often work well for those seeking morning alertness and lasting energy. By breaking the fast with a meal rich in proteins, healthy fats, and fiber, you set a stable foundation for blood sugar and prevent energy crashes later in the day.

Listening to your body's signals is key when choosing the right fasting schedule. Flexibility is essential, and adjusting your fasting window on days with a higher energy demand is completely fine. The goal is to find a rhythm that supports your natural energy flow, allowing you to feel vibrant, focused, and well-fueled.

Breakfast

37. Almond Butter & Banana Smoothie

Description: A creamy smoothie made with almond butter and banana, offering healthy fats, natural sugars, and protein for a quick, energy-boosting breakfast.

Servings: 1 | **Prep time**: 5 minutes | **Cooking time**: 0 minutes

Ingredients:

➢ 1 banana
➢ 1 tbsp almond butter
➢ 1 cup almond milk (or milk of choice)
➢ 1 tbsp chia seeds
➢ ½ tsp cinnamon
➢ ½ cup ice cubes

Preparation Steps: Combine banana, almond butter, almond milk, chia seeds, cinnamon, and ice in a blender. Blend until smooth, pour into a glass, and enjoy immediately for a delicious start to your day.

Ratings: Calories: 320 kcal | Energy Boost: 5/5 | Protein Support: 4/5 | Satiety Factor: 4/5 | Blood Sugar Stability: 4/5 | Healthy Fats: 5/5

38. Veggie & Egg Scramble with Avocado

Description: A savory scramble loaded with fresh vegetables and topped with avocado, providing protein, fiber, and healthy fats to keep energy levels steady.

Servings: 1 | **Prep time**: 5 minutes | **Cooking time**: 5 minutes

Ingredients:

➢ 2 eggs
➢ ¼ cup diced bell pepper
➢ ¼ cup diced zucchini
➢ 1 tbsp olive oil
➢ ½ avocado, sliced
➢ Salt and pepper to taste

Preparation Steps: Heat olive oil in a skillet over medium heat. Add bell pepper and zucchini, sautéing until tender. Whisk the eggs, pour into the skillet, and scramble with the vegetables until fully cooked. Serve topped with avocado slices.

Ratings: Calories: 280 kcal | Protein Support: 5/5 | Healthy Fats: 5/5 | Satiety Factor: 5/5 | Blood Sugar Stability: 4/5 | Energy Boost: 5/5

39. Oatmeal with Hemp Seeds & Fresh Fruit

Description: A classic oatmeal topped with nutrient-dense hemp seeds and fresh fruit, providing sustained energy, fiber, and plant-based protein.

Servings: 1 | **Prep time**: 5 minutes | **Cooking time**: 5 minutes

Ingredients:

➢ ½ cup rolled oats
➢ 1 cup water or milk of choice
➢ 1 tbsp hemp seeds
➢ ¼ cup sliced fresh fruit (e.g., berries, banana)
➢ 1 tsp honey (optional)

Preparation Steps: In a small pot, cook oats with water or milk over medium heat until creamy. Serve topped with hemp seeds, fresh fruit, and a drizzle of honey if desired.

Ratings: Calories: 290 kcal | Fiber Support: 5/5 | Protein Support: 4/5 | Blood Sugar Stability: 5/5 | Satiety Factor: 5/5 | Energy Boost: 4/5

40. Matcha Green Tea Smoothie

Description: A refreshing smoothie made with matcha green tea, packed with antioxidants and a gentle dose of caffeine to boost morning energy levels without jitters.

Servings: 1 | **Prep time**: 5 minutes | **Cooking time**: 0 minutes

Ingredients:

➢ 1 tsp matcha powder
➢ 1 banana
➢ 1 cup almond milk
➢ 1 tbsp chia seeds
➢ ½ cup ice cubes

Preparation Steps: Blend matcha powder, banana, almond milk, chia seeds, and ice until smooth. Enjoy immediately for a refreshing, energy-boosting start.

Ratings: Calories: 230 kcal | Antioxidant Power: 5/5 | Energy Boost: 5/5 | Blood Sugar Stability: 4/5 | Satiety Factor: 4/5 | Caffeine Balance: 4/5

41. Protein-Packed Cottage Cheese & Berry Bowl

Description: Cottage cheese topped with fresh berries and a sprinkle of seeds, offering high protein and antioxidants for a balanced, energizing breakfast.

Servings: 1 | **Prep time**: 5 minutes | **Cooking time**: 0 minutes

Ingredients:

➢ 1 cup cottage cheese
➢ ½ cup mixed berries
➢ 1 tbsp chia seeds or flaxseeds
➢ 1 tsp honey (optional)

Preparation Steps: In a bowl, top cottage cheese with berries and chia seeds, drizzling honey on top if desired. Mix and enjoy as a protein-rich, quick breakfast.

Ratings: Calories: 250 kcal | Protein Support: 5/5 | Antioxidant Power: 4/5 | Blood Sugar Stability: 5/5 | Satiety Factor: 5/5 | Energy Boost: 4/5

42. Peanut Butter & Chia Toast

Description: A simple toast topped with creamy peanut butter and chia seeds, providing healthy fats and fiber for an easy and energizing start to your morning.

Servings: 1 | **Prep time**: 5 minutes | **Cooking time**: 0 minutes

Ingredients:

➢ 1 slice whole-grain bread, toasted
➢ 1 tbsp peanut butter
➢ 1 tsp chia seeds
➢ ½ banana, sliced

Preparation Steps: Spread peanut butter on toast, top with chia seeds and banana slices, and enjoy immediately.

Ratings: Calories: 280 kcal | Fiber Support: 4/5 | Protein Support: 4/5 | Blood Sugar Stability: 4/5 | Healthy Fats: 5/5 | Energy Boost: 4/5

43. Fruit & Nut Overnight Oats

Description: A make-ahead breakfast with oats, fruits, and nuts, offering balanced macros and fiber for lasting energy and fullness.

Servings: 1 | **Prep time**: 5 minutes | **Cooking time**: 0 minutes (overnight soak)

Ingredients:

➢ ½ cup rolled oats
➢ 1 cup almond milk
➢ ¼ cup mixed berries
➢ 1 tbsp chopped almonds
➢ 1 tsp honey or maple syrup (optional)

Preparation Steps: Combine oats and almond milk in a jar, stirring well. Top with berries and almonds, cover, and refrigerate overnight. Stir and enjoy in the morning.

Ratings: Calories: 300 kcal | Fiber Support: 5/5 | Protein Support: 4/5 | Satiety Factor: 5/5 | Blood Sugar Stability: 5/5 | Energy Boost: 4/5

44. High-Protein Greek Yogurt Parfait

Description: A Greek yogurt parfait layered with berries and granola, providing a high-protein, antioxidant-rich breakfast that sustains energy levels.

Servings: 1 | **Prep time**: 5 minutes | **Cooking time**: 0 minutes

Ingredients:

➢ 1 cup Greek yogurt
➢ ½ cup mixed berries
➢ 2 tbsp granola
➢ 1 tsp honey (optional)

Preparation Steps: Layer Greek yogurt with berries and granola in a bowl or jar. Drizzle with honey if desired and enjoy immediately.

Ratings: Calories: 280 kcal | Protein Support: 5/5 | Antioxidant Power: 4/5 | Blood Sugar Stability: 5/5 | Satiety Factor: 5/5 | Energy Boost: 4/5

45. Almond & Berry Protein Smoothie

Description: This almond and berry smoothie combines protein, antioxidants, and healthy fats for an energy-sustaining breakfast.

Servings: 1 | **Prep time**: 5 minutes | **Cooking time**: 0 minutes

Ingredients:

➢ 1 cup almond milk
➢ ½ cup mixed berries
➢ 1 tbsp almond butter
➢ 1 tbsp chia seeds
➢ ½ cup ice cubes

Preparation Steps: Blend almond milk, berries, almond butter, chia seeds, and ice until smooth. Serve immediately.

Ratings: Calories: 250 kcal | Protein Support: 4/5 | Antioxidant Power: 4/5 | Blood Sugar Stability: 5/5 | Healthy Fats: 5/5 | Energy Boost: 4/5

46. Morning Energy-Boosting Muffins

Description: These whole-grain muffins are packed with nuts and seeds for a fiber-rich, energy-boosting breakfast that's perfect for on-the-go mornings.

Servings: 6 muffins | **Prep time**: 10 minutes | **Cooking time**: 20 minutes

Ingredients:

➢ 1 cup whole wheat flour
➢ 1/4 cup chopped walnuts
➢ 1/4 cup pumpkin seeds
➢ 1/2 cup applesauce
➢ 1/4 cup honey
➢ 1 tsp baking powder

Preparation Steps: Preheat oven to 350°F (175°C). Mix all ingredients in a bowl until well-combined. Divide batter into muffin tin and bake for 20 minutes. Cool and enjoy.

Ratings: Calories: 180 kcal | Fiber Support: 5/5 | Satiety Factor: 4/5 | Blood Sugar Stability: 4/5 | Energy Boost: 5/5 | Portable: 5/5

47. Banana & Almond Energy Bars

Description: Homemade energy bars with banana and almonds, packed with natural sugars, protein, and fiber for a quick, energizing breakfast.

Servings: 4 bars | **Prep time**: 10 minutes | **Cooking time**: 0 minutes

Ingredients:

- 2 ripe bananas
- 1/2 cup almond butter
- 1 cup rolled oats
- 1/4 cup chopped almonds

Preparation Steps: Mash bananas and mix with almond butter and oats until well combined. Add chopped almonds, press mixture into a baking dish, and refrigerate for 1 hour. Slice into bars.

Ratings: Calories: 210 kcal | Fiber Support: 4/5 | Satiety Factor: 4/5 | Protein Support: 4/5 | Blood Sugar Stability: 4/5 | Energy Boost: 5/5

48. Chia-Infused Green Smoothie

Description: This green smoothie with chia seeds provides a refreshing and fiber-rich breakfast that boosts energy and hydration.

Servings: 1 | **Prep time**: 5 minutes | **Cooking time**: 0 minutes

Ingredients:

- 1 cup spinach
- 1 apple, chopped
- 1 cup coconut water
- 1 tbsp chia seeds
- ½ cup ice cubes

Preparation Steps: Blend spinach, apple, coconut water, chia seeds, and ice until smooth. Serve immediately.

Ratings: Calories: 180 kcal | Hydration Support: 5/5 | Fiber Support: 4/5 | Energy Boost: 4/5 | Blood Sugar Stability: 4/5 | Antioxidant Power: 4/5

49. Mango & Spinach Protein Smoothie

Description: This tropical smoothie with mango and spinach provides antioxidants and plant-based protein for a light yet energizing breakfast.

Servings: 1 | **Prep time**: 5 minutes | **Cooking time**: 0 minutes

Ingredients:

- 1 cup spinach
- ½ cup mango chunks
- 1 cup almond milk
- 1 tbsp chia seeds
- ½ cup ice cubes

Preparation Steps: Blend spinach, mango, almond milk, chia seeds, and ice until smooth. Enjoy immediately for a tropical, energizing boost.

Ratings: Calories: 200 kcal | Antioxidant Power: 5/5 | Fiber Support: 4/5 | Blood Sugar Stability: 4/5 | Energy Boost: 5/5 | Protein Support: 3/5

Lunch

50. Quinoa & Black Bean Salad

Description: A protein-packed quinoa and black bean salad loaded with fresh veggies, offering balanced nutrients to sustain energy and keep you feeling full throughout the day.

Servings: 2 | **Prep time**: 10 minutes | **Cooking time**: 15 minutes

Ingredients:

➢ 1 cup cooked quinoa
➢ 1 cup black beans, rinsed and drained
➢ ½ cup diced bell pepper
➢ ¼ cup chopped cilantro
➢ 1 tbsp olive oil
➢ 1 tbsp lime juice
➢ Salt and pepper to taste

Preparation Steps: In a large bowl, combine quinoa, black beans, bell pepper, and cilantro. Drizzle with olive oil and lime juice, season with salt and pepper, and toss to combine. Serve immediately or refrigerate for a chilled salad.

Ratings: Calories: 320 kcal | Protein Support: 5/5 | Fiber Support: 5/5 | Blood Sugar Stability: 5/5 | Satiety Factor: 4/5 | Energy Boost: 5/5

51. Egg Salad Lettuce Wraps

Description: Light and refreshing lettuce wraps filled with protein-rich egg salad, perfect for a low-carb, energy-sustaining lunch.

Servings: 2 | **Prep time**: 10 minutes | **Cooking time**: 10 minutes

Ingredients:

➢ 4 hard-boiled eggs, chopped
➢ 2 tbsp Greek yogurt or mayo
➢ 1 tbsp Dijon mustard
➢ 1 tbsp chopped chives
➢ 6 large lettuce leaves
➢ Salt and pepper to taste

Preparation Steps: In a bowl, mix chopped eggs, Greek yogurt or mayo, Dijon mustard, and chives. Spoon the egg salad onto lettuce leaves, season with salt and pepper, and wrap tightly to serve.

Ratings: Calories: 250 kcal | Protein Support: 5/5 | Blood Sugar Stability: 5/5 | Low-Carb Option: 5/5 | Digestive Health: 4/5 | Satiety Factor: 4/5

52. Sweet Potato & Black Bean Tacos

Description: Flavorful tacos filled with roasted sweet potato and black beans, providing fiber, complex carbs, and protein for lasting energy.

Servings: 2 | **Prep time**: 10 minutes | **Cooking time**: 20 minutes

Ingredients:

- ➢ 1 medium sweet potato, cubed and roasted
- ➢ 1 cup black beans, rinsed and drained
- ➢ 4 small corn tortillas
- ➢ ¼ cup diced red onion
- ➢ 1 tbsp chopped cilantro
- ➢ 1 tbsp lime juice

Preparation Steps: Roast sweet potato cubes at 400°F (200°C) for 20 minutes until tender. In tortillas, layer sweet potato, black beans, red onion, and cilantro. Drizzle with lime juice and serve.

Ratings: Calories: 300 kcal | Fiber Support: 5/5 | Protein Support: 4/5 | Blood Sugar Stability: 4/5 | Energy Boost: 5/5 | Digestive Health: 4/5

53. Chicken & Avocado Salad

Description: A high-protein chicken and avocado salad, perfect for a filling lunch that promotes energy and keeps blood sugar stable.

Servings: 2 | **Prep time**: 10 minutes | **Cooking time**: 15 minutes

Ingredients:

- ➢ 1 cup cooked chicken breast, chopped
- ➢ 1 avocado, diced
- ➢ 2 cups mixed greens
- ➢ 1 tbsp olive oil
- ➢ 1 tbsp lemon juice
- ➢ Salt and pepper to taste

Preparation Steps: In a large bowl, combine chicken, avocado, and mixed greens. Drizzle with olive oil and lemon

juice, season with salt and pepper, and toss to coat. Serve immediately.

Ratings: Calories: 350 kcal | Protein Support: 5/5 | Healthy Fats: 5/5 | Blood Sugar Stability: 5/5 | Satiety Factor: 5/5 | Energy Boost: 5/5

54. Greek-Inspired Turkey Salad with Olives

Description: A Greek-inspired salad with lean turkey, olives, and fresh vegetables, offering a flavorful, high-protein lunch to sustain energy levels.

Servings: 2 | **Prep time**: 10 minutes | **Cooking time**: 10 minutes

Ingredients:

- ➢ 1 cup cooked turkey breast, chopped
- ➢ ¼ cup Kalamata olives, sliced
- ➢ ½ cup diced cucumber
- ➢ ½ cup cherry tomatoes, halved
- ➢ 1 tbsp olive oil
- ➢ 1 tbsp red wine vinegar

Preparation Steps: Combine turkey, olives, cucumber, and tomatoes in a bowl. Drizzle with olive oil and red wine vinegar, toss, and serve immediately.

Ratings: Calories: 320 kcal | Protein Support: 5/5 | Satiety Factor: 5/5 | Blood Sugar Stability: 5/5 | Digestive Health: 4/5 | Energy Boost: 4/5

55. Lentil Salad with Spinach & Fresh Herbs

Description: A hearty lentil salad packed with spinach and fresh herbs, delivering plant-based protein, fiber, and antioxidants for a balanced, energizing lunch.

Servings: 2 | **Prep time**: 10 minutes | **Cooking time**: 20 minutes

Ingredients:

➢ 1 cup cooked lentils
➢ 2 cups spinach
➢ ¼ cup chopped parsley
➢ 1 tbsp olive oil
➢ 1 tbsp lemon juice
➢ Salt and pepper to taste

Preparation Steps: In a bowl, combine lentils, spinach, and parsley. Drizzle with olive oil and lemon juice, season with salt and pepper, and toss to combine.

Ratings: Calories: 290 kcal | Fiber Support: 5/5 | Plant-Based Protein: 4/5 | Blood Sugar Stability: 5/5 | Digestive Health: 5/5 | Energy Boost: 4/5

56. Edamame & Mixed Greens Bowl

Description: A refreshing bowl featuring edamame and mixed greens, delivering plant-based protein, fiber, and healthy fats to sustain energy.

Servings: 2 | **Prep time**: 5 minutes | **Cooking time**: 0 minutes

Ingredients:

➢ 1 cup shelled edamame
➢ 2 cups mixed greens
➢ ¼ cup shredded carrots
➢ 1 tbsp sesame seeds
➢ 1 tbsp rice vinegar

Preparation Steps: Combine edamame, mixed greens, and carrots in a bowl. Sprinkle with sesame seeds and drizzle with rice vinegar, tossing to mix well. Serve immediately.

Ratings: Calories: 260 kcal | Protein Support: 4/5 | Fiber Support: 5/5 | Blood Sugar Stability: 5/5 | Digestive Health: 4/5 | Energy Boost: 4/5

57. Roasted Chickpea Salad with Tahini Dressing

Description: A filling salad with roasted chickpeas and a creamy tahini dressing, providing fiber, protein, and lasting energy.

Servings: 2 | **Prep time**: 10 minutes | **Cooking time**: 20 minutes

Ingredients:

➢ 1 cup canned chickpeas, rinsed and drained
➢ 2 cups mixed greens
➢ 1 tbsp olive oil
➢ 1 tbsp tahini
➢ 1 tbsp lemon juice
➢ Salt and pepper to taste

Preparation Steps: Roast chickpeas in a preheated oven at 400°F (200°C) for 20 minutes until crispy. In a bowl, toss mixed greens with roasted chickpeas, tahini, lemon juice, salt, and pepper.

Ratings: Calories: 280 kcal | Fiber Support: 5/5 | Protein Support: 4/5 | Blood Sugar Stability: 5/5 | Satiety Factor: 5/5 | Energy Boost: 4/5

58. Salmon & Avocado Energy Bowl

Description: A nutrient-rich bowl with salmon, avocado, and mixed greens, providing healthy fats, protein, and antioxidants to support sustained energy and focus.

Servings: 2 | **Prep time**: 10 minutes | **Cooking time**: 10 minutes

Ingredients:

➤ 1 cup cooked salmon, flaked
➤ 1 avocado, sliced
➤ 2 cups mixed greens
➤ 1 tbsp olive oil
➤ 1 tbsp apple cider vinegar

Preparation Steps: In a bowl, arrange mixed greens and top with salmon and avocado. Drizzle with olive oil and apple cider vinegar, tossing gently to combine. Serve immediately.

Ratings: Calories: 340 kcal | Protein Support: 5/5 | Healthy Fats: 5/5 | Blood Sugar Stability: 5/5 | Satiety Factor: 5/5 | Energy Boost: 5/5

59. Grilled Veggie & Hummus Wrap

Description: A flavorful wrap with grilled vegetables and creamy hummus, providing fiber, plant-based protein, and nutrients for lasting energy.

Servings: 1 | **Prep time**: 5 minutes | **Cooking time**: 10 minutes

Ingredients:

➤ 1 large whole-grain wrap
➤ ¼ cup hummus
➤ ½ cup grilled zucchini
➤ ¼ cup grilled bell peppers
➤ ¼ cup spinach leaves

Preparation Steps: Spread hummus on the wrap, then layer with grilled zucchini, bell peppers, and spinach. Roll tightly, slice in half, and enjoy.

Ratings: Calories: 300 kcal | Fiber Support: 5/5 | Plant-Based Protein: 4/5 | Blood Sugar Stability: 5/5 | Satiety Factor: 4/5 | Energy Boost: 4/5

60. Energizing Carrot & Cabbage Slaw

Description: A vibrant slaw made with carrots, cabbage, and a light dressing, delivering fiber and antioxidants for a refreshing, energy-supporting lunch.

Servings: 2 | **Prep time**: 10 minutes | **Cooking time**: 0 minutes

Ingredients:

➤ 1 cup shredded carrots
➤ 1 cup shredded cabbage
➤ 1 tbsp apple cider vinegar
➤ 1 tbsp olive oil
➤ Salt and pepper to taste

Preparation Steps: In a bowl, toss together shredded carrots and cabbage.

Drizzle with apple cider vinegar and olive oil, season with salt and pepper, and mix well. Serve as a light, refreshing salad.

Ratings: Calories: 180 kcal | Fiber Support: 5/5 | Antioxidant Power: 5/5 | Blood Sugar Stability: 4/5 | Digestive Health: 5/5 | Energy Boost: 3/5

61. Sautéed Zucchini & Tomato Wrap

Description: A quick and easy wrap filled with sautéed zucchini, tomatoes, and herbs, perfect for a light yet satisfying lunch.

Servings: 1 | **Prep time**: 5 minutes | **Cooking time**: 5 minutes

Ingredients:

➢ 1 large whole-grain wrap
➢ 1 small zucchini, sliced
➢ 1 small tomato, diced
➢ 1 tbsp olive oil
➢ 1 tsp dried basil

Preparation Steps: Sauté zucchini and tomatoes in olive oil over medium heat, seasoning with dried basil. Spoon into the wrap, roll tightly, and enjoy immediately.

Ratings: Calories: 250 kcal | Fiber Support: 4/5 | Blood Sugar Stability: 4/5 | Digestive Health: 4/5 | Satiety Factor: 4/5 | Energy Boost: 4/5

Dinner

62. Zucchini Noodles with Basil Pesto Chicken

Description: A light, low-carb dish with zucchini noodles and basil pesto chicken, offering healthy fats and protein to keep energy stable throughout the evening.

Servings: 2 | **Prep time**: 10 minutes | **Cooking time**: 10 minutes

Ingredients:

➢ 2 cups zucchini noodles
➢ 1 cup cooked chicken breast, sliced
➢ 2 tbsp basil pesto
➢ 1 tbsp olive oil
➢ Salt and pepper to taste

Preparation Steps: Heat olive oil in a skillet over medium heat, add zucchini noodles, and sauté for 2-3 minutes. Toss in the chicken and basil pesto, seasoning with salt and pepper. Stir until well combined, then serve immediately.

Ratings: Calories: 320 kcal | Protein Support: 5/5 | Healthy Fats: 5/5 | Low-Carb Option: 5/5 | Blood Sugar Stability: 5/5 | Energy Boost: 4/5

63. Lentil & Veggie Soup with Fresh Herbs

Description: A hearty lentil soup filled with fresh vegetables and herbs, providing fiber, plant-based protein, and a comforting dinner for sustained energy.

Servings: 2 | **Prep time**: 10 minutes | **Cooking time**: 30 minutes

Ingredients:

➢ 1 cup cooked lentils
➢ 1 carrot, diced

➢ 1 celery stalk, diced

➢ 2 cups vegetable broth

➢ 1 tbsp fresh parsley, chopped

➢ Salt and pepper to taste

Preparation Steps: In a pot, combine lentils, carrot, celery, and vegetable broth. Simmer over medium heat for 30 minutes, stirring occasionally. Add fresh parsley and season with salt and pepper before serving.

Ratings: Calories: 260 kcal | Fiber Support: 5/5 | Plant-Based Protein: 5/5 | Blood Sugar Stability: 5/5 | Digestive Health: 5/5 | Energy Boost: 4/5

64. Garlic Shrimp with Cauliflower Rice

Description: A low-carb dinner with garlic shrimp served over cauliflower rice, offering lean protein and fiber for a light and energy-sustaining meal.

Servings: 2 | **Prep time**: 5 minutes | **Cooking time**: 10 minutes

Ingredients:

➢ 1 cup shrimp, peeled and deveined

➢ 2 cups cauliflower rice

➢ 1 tbsp olive oil

➢ 2 cloves garlic, minced

➢ Salt and pepper to taste

Preparation Steps: Heat olive oil in a skillet, add garlic, and cook until fragrant. Add shrimp and cook until pink. Stir in cauliflower rice, season with salt and pepper, and cook until cauliflower is tender. Serve warm.

Ratings: Calories: 230 kcal | Protein Support: 5/5 | Low-Carb Option: 5/5 | Blood Sugar Stability: 5/5 | Satiety Factor: 4/5 | Digestive Health: 4/5

65. Stuffed Bell Peppers with Ground Turkey

Description: Bell peppers stuffed with ground turkey and spices, providing a high-protein, low-carb dinner for lasting energy and fullness.

Servings: 2 | **Prep time**: 10 minutes | **Cooking time**: 20 minutes

Ingredients:

➢ 2 large bell peppers, halved and seeded

➢ 1 cup ground turkey, cooked

➢ ¼ cup diced tomatoes

➢ 1 tbsp olive oil

➢ Salt and pepper to taste

Preparation Steps: Preheat oven to 375°F (190°C). Stuff bell peppers with ground turkey and diced tomatoes, place in a baking dish, and drizzle with olive oil. Bake for 20 minutes until peppers are tender. Serve warm.

Ratings: Calories: 290 kcal | Protein Support: 5/5 | Blood Sugar Stability: 5/5 | Satiety Factor: 5/5 | Low-Carb Option: 4/5 | Energy Boost: 4/5

66. Spinach & Tofu Stir Fry

Description: A quick and nutritious stir fry with spinach and tofu, delivering plant-based protein, iron, and fiber to support hormone health and energy.

Servings: 2 | **Prep time**: 5 minutes | **Cooking time**: 10 minutes

Ingredients:

➢ 1 cup tofu, cubed
➢ 2 cups spinach
➢ 1 tbsp soy sauce (or tamari for gluten-free)
➢ 1 tbsp olive oil
➢ Salt and pepper to taste

Preparation Steps: Heat olive oil in a skillet over medium heat. Add tofu and cook until golden brown, then add spinach and soy sauce. Stir until spinach is wilted, season with salt and pepper, and serve immediately.

Ratings: Calories: 250 kcal | Plant-Based Protein: 5/5 | Fiber Support: 4/5 | Iron Boost: 4/5 | Blood Sugar Stability: 4/5 | Energy Boost: 4/5

67. Baked Cod with Spinach & Tomatoes

Description: A light and delicious dinner with baked cod, spinach, and tomatoes, providing lean protein, antioxidants, and omega-3s for lasting energy.

Servings: 2 | **Prep time**: 5 minutes | **Cooking time**: 15 minutes

Ingredients:

➢ 2 cod fillets
➢ 2 cups spinach
➢ 1 cup cherry tomatoes, halved
➢ 1 tbsp olive oil
➢ Salt and pepper to taste

Preparation Steps: Preheat oven to 400°F (200°C). Place cod, spinach, and tomatoes in a baking dish, drizzle with olive oil, and season with salt and pepper. Bake for 15 minutes until cod is cooked through. Serve warm.

Ratings: Calories: 280 kcal | Protein Support: 5/5 | Antioxidant Power: 4/5 | Omega-3 Support: 4/5 | Blood Sugar Stability: 5/5 | Energy Boost: 4/5

68. Protein-Packed Vegetable Stew

Description: A comforting vegetable stew filled with protein-rich beans and fresh veggies, perfect for a warming and energy-sustaining dinner.

Servings: 2 | **Prep time**: 10 minutes | **Cooking time**: 30 minutes

Ingredients:

➢ 1 cup white beans, rinsed and drained
➢ 1 cup diced carrots
➢ 1 cup chopped celery
➢ 2 cups vegetable broth
➢ Salt and pepper to taste

Preparation Steps: In a pot, combine white beans, carrots, celery, and vegetable broth. Simmer for 30 minutes, stirring occasionally, until vegetables are tender. Season with salt and pepper before serving.

Ratings: Calories: 320 kcal | Fiber Support: 5/5 | Plant-Based Protein: 5/5 | Blood Sugar Stability: 5/5 | Digestive Health: 5/5 | Satiety Factor: 4/5

69. Cauliflower & Broccoli Stir Fry

Description: A quick and fiber-rich stir fry with cauliflower and broccoli, providing a light and energizing dinner packed with nutrients.

Servings: 2 | **Prep time**: 5 minutes | **Cooking time**: 10 minutes

Ingredients:

➢ 1 cup cauliflower florets
➢ 1 cup broccoli florets
➢ 1 tbsp olive oil
➢ 1 tbsp soy sauce (or tamari)
➢ Salt and pepper to taste

Preparation Steps: Heat olive oil in a skillet over medium heat. Add cauliflower and broccoli, stir-frying until tender. Drizzle with soy sauce, season with salt and pepper, and serve immediately.

Ratings: Calories: 200 kcal | Fiber Support: 5/5 | Digestive Health: 5/5 | Low-Calorie Option: 5/5 | Blood Sugar Stability: 5/5 | Energy Boost: 4/5

70. Lemon & Herb Chicken with Roasted Veggies

Description: A simple yet flavorful dish with lemon-herb chicken and roasted vegetables, providing protein and fiber for a balanced, energizing dinner.

Servings: 2 | **Prep time**: 10 minutes | **Cooking time**: 25 minutes

Ingredients:

➢ 1 chicken breast, sliced
➢ 1 tbsp lemon juice
➢ 1 tbsp fresh rosemary
➢ 1 cup diced carrots
➢ 1 cup diced zucchini
➢ 1 tbsp olive oil

Preparation Steps: Preheat oven to 400°F (200°C). Marinate chicken in lemon juice and rosemary. Place chicken, carrots, and zucchini on a baking sheet, drizzle with olive oil, and roast for 25 minutes until chicken is cooked and veggies are tender.

Ratings: Calories: 320 kcal | Protein Support: 5/5 | Fiber Support: 4/5 | Blood Sugar Stability: 5/5 | Digestive Health: 4/5 | Energy Boost: 5/5

71. Quinoa & Veggie Stuffed Zucchini Boats

Description: Zucchini boats filled with quinoa and vegetables, offering a high-fiber, protein-packed dinner for balanced energy.

Servings: 2 | **Prep time**: 10 minutes | **Cooking time**: 15 minutes

Ingredients:

➢ 2 medium zucchinis, halved and hollowed
➢ 1 cup cooked quinoa
➢ ½ cup diced tomatoes
➢ 1 tbsp fresh basil, chopped
➢ Salt and pepper to taste

Preparation Steps: Preheat oven to 375°F (190°C). Stuff zucchinis with quinoa, tomatoes, and basil. Place in a baking dish and bake for 15 minutes. Season with salt and pepper before serving.

Ratings: Calories: 300 kcal | Fiber Support: 5/5 | Plant-Based Protein: 4/5 | Blood Sugar Stability: 5/5 | Digestive Health: 5/5 | Satiety Factor: 4/5

72. Grilled Salmon with Lemon & Dill

Description: A flavorful grilled salmon dish seasoned with lemon and dill, providing protein, healthy fats, and antioxidants for a nourishing, energy-sustaining dinner.

Servings: 2 | **Prep time**: 5 minutes | **Cooking time**: 10 minutes

Ingredients:

➢ 2 salmon fillets
➢ 1 tbsp lemon juice
➢ 1 tsp dried dill
➢ Salt and pepper to taste

Preparation Steps: Preheat grill to medium heat. Season salmon with lemon juice, dill, salt, and pepper. Grill for 5-7 minutes on each side, until cooked through. Serve warm.

Ratings: Calories: 320 kcal | Protein Support: 5/5 | Omega-3 Support: 5/5 | Blood Sugar Stability: 5/5 | Satiety Factor: 5/5 | Antioxidant Power: 4/5

73. Chickpea & Turmeric Casserole

Description: A warm and comforting chickpea casserole with turmeric, providing anti-inflammatory support and plant-based protein for a balanced, nourishing dinner.

Servings: 2 | **Prep time**: 10 minutes | **Cooking time**: 30 minutes

Ingredients:

➢ 1 cup chickpeas, rinsed and drained
➢ 1 cup diced carrots
➢ 1 cup spinach
➢ 1 tsp turmeric powder
➢ 1 cup vegetable broth

Preparation Steps: Preheat oven to 375°F (190°C). In a baking dish, combine chickpeas, carrots, spinach, turmeric, and vegetable broth. Bake for 30 minutes until vegetables are tender and flavors meld.

Ratings: Calories: 280 kcal | Fiber Support: 5/5 | Plant-Based Protein: 5/5 | Anti-Inflammatory Support: 5/5 | Digestive Health: 5/5 | Satiety Factor: 4/5

Chapter 3: Recipes for Sustainable Weight Loss

Achieving sustainable weight loss is often about more than simply reducing calories; it involves nourishing your body with the right balance of nutrients to support metabolism and maintain energy throughout the day. This chapter focuses on low-calorie, high-fiber recipes designed to promote satiety, manage blood sugar, and boost metabolism without sacrificing flavor. Each meal is packed with ingredients that help reduce cravings, keep energy stable, and support healthy digestion, all crucial elements in maintaining a sustainable approach to weight loss.

This chapter also includes practical tips on using fasting as a tool for weight loss. When incorporated thoughtfully, fasting can be an effective method for reducing caloric intake, supporting metabolic health, and promoting fat loss without feeling deprived. By choosing the best fasting schedules and learning how to stay satiated on fasting days, you'll be able to manage hunger while reaching your weight loss goals comfortably.

Fasting for Weight Loss

Fasting can be a valuable tool for weight loss when paired with nutrient-dense, low-calorie meals. While fasting doesn't necessarily change what you eat, it optimizes the timing of meals, helping to create a natural calorie deficit that supports weight management. By understanding the best fasting schedules for weight loss and incorporating strategies to stay satiated, you can benefit from fasting without compromising your energy levels or overall well-being.

Best Fasting Schedules for Weight Loss

When it comes to fasting for weight loss, schedules like the 16:8 and the 5:2 are among the most effective. The 16:8 fasting schedule involves a 16-hour fasting period followed by an 8-hour eating window, typically allowing for two meals and one snack. This approach creates a natural calorie reduction by condensing meals into a smaller window, while still providing sufficient time for nutrient-dense meals. It's also relatively easy to maintain, as the majority of the fasting period takes place overnight, making it a flexible option that fits into most lifestyles.

The 5:2 fasting schedule, on the other hand, involves eating normally for five days of the week and limiting intake to about 500–600 calories on two non-consecutive days. This method can be particularly beneficial for those who prefer flexibility, as it allows for a more relaxed eating schedule on most days. By reducing caloric intake on two specific days, you create a weekly calorie deficit that supports weight loss while still allowing for nutrient-dense meals on fasting days.

For individuals seeking a gentle approach, the 14:10 schedule—where you fast for 14 hours and eat within a 10-hour window—can also be effective. While the caloric impact may be smaller, it still provides benefits to metabolism and blood sugar stability, and it's especially suitable for those new to fasting.

Tips for Staying Satiated on Fasting Days

Staying satiated on fasting days is essential for making fasting a sustainable practice. One of the best strategies is to focus on high-fiber, water-rich foods during eating periods, such as leafy greens, berries, cucumbers, and soups. These foods are naturally low in calories but add bulk to meals, keeping you full longer. Healthy fats from sources like avocado, nuts, and seeds are also beneficial, as they provide sustained energy and help reduce hunger during fasting hours.

Timing your meals to coincide with the start of your fasting period can also make a big difference. Having your last meal rich in protein, fiber, and healthy fats before beginning a fast can help stabilize blood sugar and curb cravings, ensuring that you don't experience extreme hunger early into the fasting period.

Hydration plays a critical role as well. Drinking plenty of water, herbal teas, and even water infused with a splash of lemon or cucumber can stave off hunger and prevent dehydration, which often masks itself as hunger. Finally, keeping busy and distracted during fasting hours can help shift focus away from food, allowing you to stay productive and committed to your weight loss goals.

By combining these fasting strategies with low-calorie, high-fiber meals from this chapter, you can maintain energy levels, avoid cravings, and support sustainable weight loss effectively and enjoyably.

Breakfast

74. Low-Calorie Berry & Almond Smoothie

Description: A refreshing smoothie made with berries and almond milk, offering a light, low-calorie start to your day while keeping you full with fiber and antioxidants.

Servings: 1 | **Prep time**: 5 minutes | **Cooking time**: 0 minutes

Ingredients:

➢ 1 cup mixed berries
➢ 1 cup unsweetened almond milk
➢ 1 tbsp chia seeds
➢ 1 tsp almond butter

Preparation Steps: Blend mixed berries, almond milk, chia seeds, and almond butter until smooth. Serve immediately for a light, nutritious breakfast.

Ratings: Calories: 180 kcal | Satiety Factor: 4/5 | Antioxidant Power: 5/5 |

Low-Calorie Option: 5/5 | Blood Sugar Stability: 4/5 | Digestive Health: 4/5

75. High-Protein Greek Yogurt & Chia Bowl

Description: This high-protein yogurt bowl with chia seeds is perfect for sustained energy and supports metabolism with a mix of fiber and probiotics.

Servings: 1 | **Prep time**: 5 minutes | **Cooking time**: 0 minutes

Ingredients:

- 1 cup Greek yogurt
- 1 tbsp chia seeds
- ½ cup fresh berries
- 1 tsp honey (optional)

Preparation Steps: Combine Greek yogurt and chia seeds in a bowl. Top with fresh berries and a drizzle of honey if desired. Mix and enjoy.

Ratings: Calories: 220 kcal | Protein Support: 5/5 | Satiety Factor: 5/5 | Blood Sugar Stability: 4/5 | Digestive Health: 5/5 | Energy Boost: 4/5

76. Avocado & Smoked Salmon Plate

Description: A low-carb breakfast featuring smoked salmon and avocado, rich in healthy fats and protein to keep you full and energized.

Servings: 1 | **Prep time**: 5 minutes | **Cooking time**: 0 minutes

Ingredients:

- ½ avocado, sliced
- 2 oz smoked salmon
- 1 tbsp capers
- 1 tbsp fresh dill

Preparation Steps: Arrange sliced avocado and smoked salmon on a plate. Garnish with capers and dill, then enjoy.

Ratings: Calories: 200 kcal | Protein Support: 4/5 | Healthy Fats: 5/5 | Satiety Factor: 5/5 | Low-Carb Option: 5/5 | Blood Sugar Stability: 5/5

77. Cinnamon-Spiced Overnight Oats

Description: Overnight oats with cinnamon and almond milk, providing a satisfying breakfast that's fiber-rich and metabolism-friendly.

Servings: 1 | **Prep time**: 5 minutes | **Cooking time**: 0 minutes (overnight soak)

Ingredients:

- ½ cup rolled oats
- 1 cup almond milk
- ½ tsp cinnamon
- 1 tsp honey (optional)

Preparation Steps: Mix oats, almond milk, and cinnamon in a jar. Cover and refrigerate overnight. Stir and enjoy in the morning.

Ratings: Calories: 180 kcal | Fiber Support: 5/5 | Satiety Factor: 5/5 | Blood Sugar Stability: 4/5 | Digestive Health: 5/5 | Low-Calorie Option: 4/5

78. Low-Carb Cauliflower & Cheese Frittata

Description: A low-carb, cheesy frittata with cauliflower, providing a satisfying breakfast that supports metabolism without the carbs.

Servings: 2 | **Prep time**: 5 minutes | **Cooking time**: 15 minutes

Ingredients:

➢ 1 cup cauliflower florets, chopped
➢ 4 eggs
➢ ¼ cup shredded cheese
➢ Salt and pepper to taste

Preparation Steps: Preheat oven to 375°F (190°C). In a bowl, whisk eggs and add cauliflower and cheese. Pour into a greased baking dish and bake for 15 minutes until set.

Ratings: Calories: 210 kcal | Protein Support: 5/5 | Low-Carb Option: 5/5 | Satiety Factor: 5/5 | Digestive Health: 4/5 | Blood Sugar Stability: 4/5

79. Spinach & Feta Egg Muffins

Description: Portable egg muffins with spinach and feta, packed with protein and fiber to support sustained energy and fullness.

Servings: 6 muffins | **Prep time**: 10 minutes | **Cooking time**: 15 minutes

Ingredients:

➢ 6 eggs
➢ 1 cup spinach, chopped
➢ ¼ cup feta cheese, crumbled

Preparation Steps: Preheat oven to 350°F (175°C). In a bowl, whisk eggs and add spinach and feta. Pour into muffin tins and bake for 15 minutes.

Ratings: Calories: 90 kcal per muffin | Protein Support: 5/5 | Fiber Support: 4/5 | Satiety Factor: 5/5 | Portable: 5/5 | Blood Sugar Stability: 5/5

80. Keto-Friendly Nut Butter Smoothie

Description: A creamy, keto-friendly smoothie made with nut butter, providing healthy fats and protein to keep you full and satisfied.

Servings: 1 | **Prep time**: 5 minutes | **Cooking time**: 0 minutes

Ingredients:

➢ 1 tbsp almond or peanut butter
➢ 1 cup unsweetened almond milk
➢ 1 tbsp chia seeds
➢ ½ cup ice cubes

Preparation Steps: Blend almond butter, almond milk, chia seeds, and ice until smooth. Enjoy immediately.

Ratings: Calories: 220 kcal | Healthy Fats: 5/5 | Protein Support: 4/5 | Low-Carb Option: 5/5 | Satiety Factor: 5/5 | Energy Boost: 4/5

81. Cucumber & Dill Yogurt Bowl

Description: A refreshing, low-calorie yogurt bowl with cucumber and dill, offering probiotics and hydration for a light, energizing breakfast.

Servings: 1 | **Prep time**: 5 minutes | **Cooking time**: 0 minutes

Ingredients:

➢ 1 cup Greek yogurt
➢ ½ cucumber, diced
➢ 1 tbsp fresh dill, chopped

Preparation Steps: Mix Greek yogurt with cucumber and dill in a bowl. Serve immediately for a cool, hydrating breakfast.

Ratings: Calories: 150 kcal | Low-Calorie Option: 5/5 | Protein Support: 5/5 | Digestive Health: 5/5 | Blood Sugar Stability: 5/5 | Satiety Factor: 4/5

82. Chia Seed Pudding with Almond Milk

Description: A simple, fiber-rich chia seed pudding that's low-calorie and filling, perfect for promoting digestion and satiety.

Servings: 1 | **Prep time**: 5 minutes | **Cooking time**: 0 minutes (overnight soak)

Ingredients:

➢ 3 tbsp chia seeds
➢ 1 cup unsweetened almond milk
➢ 1 tsp vanilla extract

Preparation Steps: Combine chia seeds, almond milk, and vanilla extract in a jar.

Stir, cover, and refrigerate overnight. Enjoy in the morning.

Ratings: Calories: 180 kcal | Fiber Support: 5/5 | Satiety Factor: 5/5 | Blood Sugar Stability: 4/5 | Digestive Health: 5/5 | Low-Calorie Option: 4/5

83. Spinach & Mushroom Omelette

Description: A light, high-protein omelette with spinach and mushrooms, offering essential nutrients and fiber for sustained energy.

Servings: 1 | **Prep time**: 5 minutes | **Cooking time**: 5 minutes

Ingredients:

➢ 2 eggs
➢ ¼ cup spinach, chopped
➢ ¼ cup mushrooms, sliced
➢ Salt and pepper to taste

Preparation Steps: Sauté mushrooms and spinach in a skillet until tender. Whisk eggs and pour over veggies, cooking until set. Serve hot.

Ratings: Calories: 180 kcal | Protein Support: 5/5 | Fiber Support: 4/5 | Satiety Factor: 5/5 | Blood Sugar Stability: 4/5 | Energy Boost: 4/5

84. Quick Almond & Blueberry Bowl

Description: A quick, low-calorie bowl with Greek yogurt, almonds, and blueberries, perfect for a high-protein, fiber-rich breakfast that supports metabolism.

Servings: 1 | **Prep time**: 5 minutes | **Cooking time**: 0 minutes

Ingredients:

➤ 1 cup Greek yogurt
➤ ¼ cup blueberries
➤ 1 tbsp sliced almonds

Preparation Steps: Combine Greek yogurt, blueberries, and almonds in a bowl. Serve immediately for a quick and energizing breakfast.

Ratings: Calories: 190 kcal | Protein Support: 5/5 | Fiber Support: 4/5 | Low-Calorie Option: 5/5 | Antioxidant Power: 4/5 | Blood Sugar Stability: 4/5

85. Coconut & Flax Oatmeal

Description: A creamy oatmeal with coconut and flax, providing fiber and healthy fats to support digestion and sustained energy.

Servings: 1 | **Prep time**: 5 minutes | **Cooking time**: 5 minutes

Ingredients:

➤ ½ cup rolled oats
➤ 1 cup coconut milk
➤ 1 tbsp flaxseeds
➤ 1 tsp shredded coconut

Preparation Steps: Cook oats with coconut milk over medium heat until creamy. Stir in flaxseeds and top with shredded coconut.

Ratings: Calories: 220 kcal | Fiber Support: 5/5 | Healthy Fats: 4/5 | Satiety

Factor: 5/5 | Blood Sugar Stability: 4/5 | Digestive Health: 5/5

86. Orange & Hemp Protein Shake

Description: A refreshing orange and hemp shake packed with protein and fiber, supporting metabolism and energy levels with minimal calories.

Servings: 1 | **Prep time**: 5 minutes | **Cooking time**: 0 minutes

Ingredients:

➤ 1 orange, peeled and segmented
➤ 1 cup almond milk
➤ 1 tbsp hemp seeds
➤ ½ cup ice cubes

Preparation Steps: Blend orange, almond milk, hemp seeds, and ice until smooth. Serve immediately for a light, refreshing start to your day.

Ratings: Calories: 180 kcal | Protein Support: 4/5 | Fiber Support: 4/5 | Low-Calorie Option: 5/5 | Blood Sugar Stability: 5/5 | Digestive Health: 4/5

Lunch

87. Turkey Lettuce Wraps with Veggies

Description: These low-carb turkey lettuce wraps are packed with lean protein and fresh veggies, making for a light yet satisfying lunch.

Servings: 2 | **Prep time**: 10 minutes | **Cooking time**: 5 minutes

Ingredients:

- 1 cup cooked ground turkey
- 1 carrot, shredded
- ¼ cup diced bell pepper
- 8 large lettuce leaves
- 1 tbsp hoisin or soy sauce

Preparation Steps: In a bowl, mix cooked ground turkey with shredded carrot, bell pepper, and hoisin or soy sauce. Spoon mixture onto lettuce leaves, wrap, and serve immediately.

Ratings: Calories: 180 kcal | Protein Support: 5/5 | Low-Carb Option: 5/5 | Blood Sugar Stability: 4/5 | Satiety Factor: 4/5 | Energy Boost: 4/5

88. Avocado & Shrimp Salad

Description: A refreshing salad with creamy avocado and shrimp, delivering protein and healthy fats for a satisfying, metabolism-supporting lunch.

Servings: 2 | **Prep time**: 10 minutes | **Cooking time**: 5 minutes

Ingredients:

- 1 cup cooked shrimp, chopped
- 1 avocado, diced
- 2 cups mixed greens
- 1 tbsp lemon juice
- Salt and pepper to taste

Preparation Steps: In a large bowl, combine shrimp, avocado, and mixed greens. Drizzle with lemon juice, season with salt and pepper, and toss to combine. Serve immediately.

Ratings: Calories: 220 kcal | Healthy Fats: 5/5 | Protein Support: 4/5 | Blood Sugar Stability: 5/5 | Satiety Factor: 5/5 | Low-Carb Option: 5/5

89. Cauliflower Rice Stir Fry

Description: A low-calorie, veggie-packed stir fry with cauliflower rice, perfect for a light yet filling lunch that supports weight loss goals.

Servings: 2 | **Prep time**: 5 minutes | **Cooking time**: 10 minutes

Ingredients:

- 2 cups cauliflower rice
- ½ cup diced bell pepper
- ½ cup shredded carrots
- 1 tbsp soy sauce
- 1 tsp sesame oil

Preparation Steps: Heat sesame oil in a skillet, add cauliflower rice, bell pepper, and carrots, stir-frying until tender. Drizzle with soy sauce and serve hot.

Ratings: Calories: 150 kcal | Low-Calorie Option: 5/5 | Fiber Support: 4/5 | Blood Sugar Stability: 4/5 | Satiety Factor: 4/5 | Digestive Health: 4/5

90. Tuna Salad with Dill & Cucumber

Description: A light tuna salad with fresh cucumber and dill, providing lean protein and healthy fats for a refreshing, low-calorie lunch.

Servings: 2 | **Prep time**: 5 minutes | **Cooking time**: 0 minutes

Ingredients:

➢ 1 can tuna, drained
➢ ½ cucumber, diced
➢ 1 tbsp Greek yogurt
➢ 1 tsp fresh dill, chopped
➢ Salt and pepper to taste

Preparation Steps: In a bowl, mix tuna, cucumber, Greek yogurt, and dill. Season with salt and pepper and serve on its own or over greens.

Ratings: Calories: 180 kcal | Protein Support: 5/5 | Low-Calorie Option: 5/5 | Satiety Factor: 4/5 | Blood Sugar Stability: 5/5 | Digestive Health: 4/5

91. Roasted Veggie & Lentil Bowl

Description: A hearty bowl filled with roasted vegetables and protein-packed lentils, perfect for a filling and energy-sustaining lunch.

Servings: 2 | **Prep time**: 10 minutes | **Cooking time**: 20 minutes

Ingredients:

➢ 1 cup cooked lentils
➢ 1 cup roasted mixed vegetables (e.g., bell pepper, zucchini, carrots)
➢ 1 tbsp olive oil
➢ Salt and pepper to taste

Preparation Steps: Toss mixed vegetables with olive oil, salt, and pepper,

and roast at 400°F (200°C) for 20 minutes. Combine with cooked lentils and serve.

Ratings: Calories: 280 kcal | Fiber Support: 5/5 | Protein Support: 5/5 | Blood Sugar Stability: 5/5 | Satiety Factor: 5/5 | Digestive Health: 5/5

92. Kale Salad with Roasted Sweet Potatoes

Description: A nutrient-dense salad with kale and roasted sweet potatoes, providing fiber, vitamins, and complex carbs for a balanced lunch.

Servings: 2 | **Prep time**: 10 minutes | **Cooking time**: 15 minutes

Ingredients:

➢ 2 cups kale, chopped
➢ 1 cup roasted sweet potato cubes
➢ 1 tbsp olive oil
➢ 1 tbsp balsamic vinegar
➢ Salt and pepper to taste

Preparation Steps: Massage chopped kale with olive oil and balsamic vinegar until tender. Toss with roasted sweet potatoes, season with salt and pepper, and serve.

Ratings: Calories: 240 kcal | Fiber Support: 5/5 | Blood Sugar Stability: 5/5 | Antioxidant Power: 4/5 | Satiety Factor: 4/5 | Digestive Health: 4/5

93. Chickpea & Spinach Protein Salad

Description: A filling salad with chickpeas and spinach, providing plant-based protein and fiber for a satisfying, weight-loss-friendly meal.

Servings: 2 | **Prep time**: 10 minutes | **Cooking time**: 0 minutes

Ingredients:

➢ 1 cup chickpeas, rinsed and drained
➢ 2 cups spinach
➢ ¼ cup diced tomatoes
➢ 1 tbsp lemon juice
➢ Salt and pepper to taste

Preparation Steps: In a bowl, combine chickpeas, spinach, and tomatoes. Drizzle with lemon juice, season with salt and pepper, and toss to combine. Serve immediately.

Ratings: Calories: 210 kcal | Plant-Based Protein: 5/5 | Fiber Support: 5/5 | Blood Sugar Stability: 5/5 | Satiety Factor: 4/5 | Digestive Health: 5/5

94. Zucchini Noodle Bowl with Fresh Basil

Description: A light and refreshing zucchini noodle bowl with fresh basil, perfect for a low-carb, high-fiber lunch.

Servings: 2 | **Prep time**: 5 minutes | **Cooking time**: 5 minutes

Ingredients:

➢ 2 cups zucchini noodles
➢ ½ cup cherry tomatoes, halved
➢ 1 tbsp olive oil
➢ 1 tbsp fresh basil, chopped
➢ Salt and pepper to taste

Preparation Steps: Heat olive oil in a skillet, add zucchini noodles and cherry tomatoes, sautéing for 2-3 minutes. Remove from heat, toss with fresh basil, season with salt and pepper, and serve.

Ratings: Calories: 150 kcal | Low-Carb Option: 5/5 | Fiber Support: 4/5 | Blood Sugar Stability: 4/5 | Digestive Health: 4/5 | Energy Boost: 3/5

95. Cabbage & Carrot Slaw with Chicken

Description: A refreshing slaw with cabbage, carrots, and lean chicken, offering protein, fiber, and crunch for a satisfying, low-calorie lunch.

Servings: 2 | **Prep time**: 10 minutes | **Cooking time**: 5 minutes

Ingredients:

➢ 1 cup cooked chicken breast, shredded
➢ 1 cup shredded cabbage
➢ 1 carrot, shredded
➢ 1 tbsp apple cider vinegar
➢ Salt and pepper to taste

Preparation Steps: In a bowl, mix shredded chicken, cabbage, and carrot. Drizzle with apple cider vinegar, season with salt and pepper, and toss to combine.

Ratings: Calories: 200 kcal | Protein Support: 5/5 | Fiber Support: 4/5 | Blood Sugar Stability: 5/5 | Satiety Factor: 4/5 | Digestive Health: 4/5

96. Asian-Inspired Tofu Salad

Description: A light, Asian-inspired salad with tofu, mixed greens, and sesame dressing, perfect for a plant-based, low-calorie lunch.

Servings: 2 | **Prep time**: 10 minutes | **Cooking time**: 5 minutes

Ingredients:

➢ 1 cup cubed tofu, cooked
➢ 2 cups mixed greens
➢ 1 tbsp sesame oil
➢ 1 tbsp soy sauce
➢ 1 tsp sesame seeds

Preparation Steps: In a bowl, combine tofu and mixed greens. Drizzle with sesame oil and soy sauce, sprinkle with sesame seeds, and toss to combine. Serve immediately.

Ratings: Calories: 210 kcal | Plant-Based Protein: 5/5 | Low-Calorie Option: 5/5 | Digestive Health: 4/5 | Blood Sugar Stability: 4/5 | Satiety Factor: 4/5

97. Low-Calorie Avocado & Microgreens Wrap

Description: A light wrap with avocado and fresh microgreens, providing healthy fats and fiber in a low-calorie, nutritious lunch.

Servings: 1 | **Prep time**: 5 minutes | **Cooking time**: 0 minutes

Ingredients:

➢ 1 large whole-grain wrap
➢ ½ avocado, sliced
➢ ¼ cup microgreens
➢ 1 tbsp hummus

Preparation Steps: Spread hummus on the wrap, layer with avocado slices and microgreens, and roll tightly. Serve immediately for a quick, satisfying lunch.

Ratings: Calories: 220 kcal | Fiber Support: 4/5 | Healthy Fats: 4/5 | Blood Sugar Stability: 5/5 | Satiety Factor: 4/5 | Low-Calorie Option: 5/5

Dinner

98. Lemon Chicken with Steamed Broccoli

Description: A simple, low-calorie lemon chicken served with steamed broccoli, providing protein and fiber to keep you full and energized.

Servings: 2 | **Prep time**: 5 minutes | **Cooking time**: 15 minutes

Ingredients:

➢ 1 chicken breast, sliced
➢ 1 tbsp lemon juice
➢ 1 tsp olive oil
➢ 2 cups broccoli florets, steamed
➢ Salt and pepper to taste

Preparation Steps: Season chicken breast with lemon juice, salt, and pepper. Heat olive oil in a skillet over medium heat and cook chicken until golden and cooked through. Serve alongside steamed broccoli.

Ratings: Calories: 250 kcal | Protein Support: 5/5 | Low-Calorie Option: 5/5 | Satiety Factor: 4/5 | Digestive Health: 4/5 | Blood Sugar Stability: 4/5

99. Low-Calorie Vegetable Stir Fry

Description: A quick, light stir fry featuring a mix of colorful vegetables, ideal for a low-calorie, fiber-rich dinner that's both filling and nutritious.

Servings: 2 | **Prep time**: 5 minutes | **Cooking time**: 10 minutes

Ingredients:

➢ 1 cup broccoli florets
➢ ½ cup bell peppers, sliced
➢ ½ cup mushrooms, sliced
➢ 1 tbsp soy sauce
➢ 1 tsp sesame oil

Preparation Steps: Heat sesame oil in a skillet over medium heat, add vegetables, and stir-fry until tender-crisp. Drizzle with soy sauce, stir well, and serve immediately.

Ratings: Calories: 150 kcal | Fiber Support: 5/5 | Low-Calorie Option: 5/5 | Digestive Health: 5/5 | Blood Sugar Stability: 4/5 | Antioxidant Power: 4/5

100. Spaghetti Squash & Turkey Meatballs

Description: A deliciously light twist on pasta, featuring spaghetti squash and lean turkey meatballs, providing a low-carb, high-protein dinner.

Servings: 2 | **Prep time**: 10 minutes | **Cooking time**: 20 minutes

Ingredients:

➢ 1 small spaghetti squash, cooked and shredded
➢ 1 cup ground turkey, formed into meatballs
➢ 1 cup marinara sauce (low-sugar)
➢ 1 tbsp olive oil
➢ Salt and pepper to taste

Preparation Steps: Cook the turkey meatballs in olive oil over medium heat until golden. Add marinara sauce and simmer. Serve over spaghetti squash.

Ratings: Calories: 320 kcal | Protein Support: 5/5 | Low-Carb Option: 5/5 | Satiety Factor: 5/5 | Blood Sugar Stability: 5/5 | Fiber Support: 4/5

101. Grilled Salmon & Asparagus with Lemon

Description: A simple, protein-rich dinner of grilled salmon and asparagus, enhanced with lemon for a refreshing, nutrient-dense meal.

Servings: 2 | **Prep time**: 5 minutes | **Cooking time**: 10 minutes

Ingredients:

➢ 2 salmon fillets
➢ 1 bunch asparagus, trimmed
➢ 1 tbsp olive oil
➢ 1 tbsp lemon juice
➢ Salt and pepper to taste

Preparation Steps: Drizzle salmon and asparagus with olive oil and lemon juice, season with salt and pepper, and grill until salmon is flaky and asparagus is tender.

Ratings: Calories: 300 kcal | Protein Support: 5/5 | Omega-3 Support: 5/5 | Satiety Factor: 5/5 | Low-Calorie Option: 4/5 | Blood Sugar Stability: 5/5

102. Roasted Brussels Sprouts with Chicken Sausage

Description: A balanced, low-calorie meal featuring roasted Brussels sprouts and lean chicken sausage, perfect for a hearty yet healthy dinner.

Servings: 2 | **Prep time**: 5 minutes | **Cooking time**: 20 minutes

Ingredients:

➢ 1 cup Brussels sprouts, halved
➢ 2 chicken sausages, sliced
➢ 1 tbsp olive oil
➢ Salt and pepper to taste

Preparation Steps: Toss Brussels sprouts with olive oil, salt, and pepper. Roast at 400°F (200°C) for 15 minutes, then add chicken sausage slices and roast for 5 more minutes.

Ratings: Calories: 280 kcal | Protein Support: 4/5 | Fiber Support: 5/5 | Satiety Factor: 4/5 | Blood Sugar Stability: 4/5 | Low-Calorie Option: 4/5

103. Sautéed Shrimp with Mixed Veggies

Description: A quick, protein-packed dinner with shrimp and a mix of colorful vegetables, providing essential nutrients without the calories.

Servings: 2 | **Prep time**: 5 minutes | **Cooking time**: 10 minutes

Ingredients:

➢ 1 cup shrimp, peeled and deveined
➢ ½ cup bell peppers, sliced
➢ ½ cup zucchini, sliced
➢ 1 tbsp olive oil
➢ Salt and pepper to taste

Preparation Steps: Heat olive oil in a skillet, add shrimp and vegetables, and sauté until shrimp is pink and veggies are tender. Season and serve immediately.

Ratings: Calories: 240 kcal | Protein Support: 5/5 | Low-Calorie Option: 5/5 | Satiety Factor: 4/5 | Digestive Health: 4/5 | Blood Sugar Stability: 4/5

104. White Fish with Fresh Herbs & Spinach

Description: A light and delicate white fish paired with fresh herbs and spinach, ideal for a high-protein, low-calorie dinner that supports metabolism.

Servings: 2 | **Prep time**: 5 minutes | **Cooking time**: 10 minutes

Ingredients:

➢ 2 white fish fillets (e.g., cod or tilapia)
➢ 2 cups spinach
➢ 1 tbsp fresh parsley, chopped

> 1 tbsp lemon juice
> Salt and pepper to taste

Preparation Steps: Season fish with lemon juice, salt, and pepper, and pan-sear over medium heat until cooked. Wilt spinach in the same pan, adding parsley at the end. Serve together.

Ratings: Calories: 220 kcal | Protein Support: 5/5 | Low-Calorie Option: 5/5 | Blood Sugar Stability: 5/5 | Digestive Health: 4/5 | Satiety Factor: 4/5

105. Cauliflower Pizza with Veggie Toppings

Description: A low-carb pizza with a cauliflower crust topped with a variety of fresh vegetables, perfect for a guilt-free, filling dinner.

Servings: 2 | **Prep time**: 15 minutes | **Cooking time**: 20 minutes

Ingredients:

> 1 small cauliflower, grated
> 1 egg
> ¼ cup shredded mozzarella
> ½ cup assorted veggies (e.g., bell peppers, mushrooms, tomatoes)
> Salt and pepper to taste

Preparation Steps: Preheat oven to 400°F (200°C). Mix cauliflower, egg, and mozzarella, form into a crust, and bake for 10 minutes. Add veggies and bake another 10 minutes.

Ratings: Calories: 280 kcal | Low-Carb Option: 5/5 | Fiber Support: 4/5 | Satiety

Factor: 5/5 | Blood Sugar Stability: 5/5 | Digestive Health: 4/5

106. Eggplant & Zucchini Stir Fry

Description: A light, veggie-packed stir fry with eggplant and zucchini, offering fiber, nutrients, and flavor in a low-calorie meal.

Servings: 2 | **Prep time**: 5 minutes | **Cooking time**: 10 minutes

Ingredients:

> 1 cup diced eggplant
> 1 cup sliced zucchini
> 1 tbsp olive oil
> 1 tsp soy sauce (optional)
> Salt and pepper to taste

Preparation Steps: Heat olive oil in a skillet, add eggplant and zucchini, and stir-fry until tender. Drizzle with soy sauce, season with salt and pepper, and serve.

Ratings: Calories: 160 kcal | Low-Calorie Option: 5/5 | Fiber Support: 4/5 | Satiety Factor: 4/5 | Digestive Health: 5/5 | Blood Sugar Stability: 4/5

107. Grilled Veggie Kebabs with Lean Beef

Description: A balanced, high-protein dinner featuring lean beef and grilled vegetable kebabs, perfect for a satisfying yet light meal.

Servings: 2 | **Prep time**: 10 minutes | **Cooking time**: 10 minutes

Ingredients:

➤ 1 cup lean beef cubes
➤ 1 cup bell peppers, zucchini, and onion, cubed
➤ 1 tbsp olive oil
➤ Salt and pepper to taste

Preparation Steps: Thread beef and veggies onto skewers, drizzle with olive oil, and season. Grill for 10 minutes until beef is cooked through and veggies are tender.

Ratings: Calories: 300 kcal | Protein Support: 5/5 | Fiber Support: 4/5 | Satiety Factor: 5/5 | Blood Sugar Stability: 4/5 | Low-Calorie Option: 4/5

108. Light Stuffed Portobello Mushrooms

Description: Hearty portobello mushrooms stuffed with a mixture of vegetables and cheese, providing a high-fiber, low-calorie dinner option.

Servings: 2 | **Prep time**: 10 minutes | **Cooking time**: 15 minutes

Ingredients:

➤ 2 large portobello mushrooms, stems removed
➤ ¼ cup diced tomatoes
➤ ¼ cup spinach, chopped
➤ ¼ cup shredded mozzarella
➤ Salt and pepper to taste

Preparation Steps: Preheat oven to 375°F (190°C). Fill mushrooms with tomatoes, spinach, and mozzarella. Bake for 15 minutes until cheese is melted and mushrooms are tender.

Ratings: Calories: 220 kcal | Fiber Support: 5/5 | Low-Calorie Option: 5/5 | Satiety Factor: 4/5 | Digestive Health: 5/5 | Blood Sugar Stability: 4/5

Chapter 4: Recipes for Gut Health

A healthy gut is essential for overall wellness, influencing everything from digestion to immunity and mental clarity. This chapter is dedicated to recipes that support optimal gut health, emphasizing ingredients rich in fiber, prebiotics, and probiotics. By incorporating these elements into your diet, you can nourish beneficial gut bacteria, promote better digestion, enhance nutrient absorption, and maintain a balanced microbiome. With recipes that are both delicious and beneficial for gut health, you can enjoy meals that not only taste great but also support a thriving digestive system.

Alongside these gut-supporting recipes, this chapter provides practical fasting tips focused on nurturing the gut. Fasting can have both positive and challenging effects on gut health, and knowing how to balance prebiotic and probiotic intake during eating windows can make a significant difference. The tips provided will guide you in incorporating gut-friendly foods into your fasting routine and in supporting your digestive system while fasting.

Gut Health Tips

Maintaining gut health during fasting requires special attention to the types of foods you consume during your eating window. Including prebiotics and probiotics in your meals not only aids digestion but also helps preserve the delicate balance of your gut microbiome. These gut health tips offer practical ways to incorporate beneficial foods into your diet, particularly around fasting, to ensure your digestive system remains supported and resilient.

Probiotic & Prebiotic Fasting Tips

Prebiotics and probiotics play complementary roles in gut health. Prebiotics, found in fiber-rich foods like onions, garlic, bananas, and asparagus, act as food for beneficial bacteria. Probiotics, on the other hand, are live bacteria found in fermented foods such as yogurt, kefir, sauerkraut, and kimchi. When consumed together, these two types of nutrients create a symbiotic relationship that enhances gut health and ensures beneficial bacteria thrive.

During fasting, it's essential to incorporate these gut-supporting foods when you break your fast. Starting with a small amount of probiotic-rich food, like a spoonful of yogurt or a sip of kefir, helps introduce beneficial bacteria to your digestive system gently, preparing it for further digestion. Following this with a fiber-rich meal that includes prebiotic foods will provide the fuel needed for these bacteria to flourish. By making this a regular practice, you can support gut health during fasting periods and enhance your body's natural ability to maintain a balanced microbiome.

Supporting Gut Health During Fasting

Fasting gives your digestive system a break, but it can also disrupt gut health if not managed carefully. To support your gut during fasting, ensure you're consuming hydrating fluids like water, herbal teas, or diluted lemon water to keep your digestive system hydrated. When breaking your fast, focus on easy-to-digest foods that are high in fiber and low in processed sugars, which can disrupt gut bacteria balance.

A gentle, gut-friendly way to break your fast is with a smoothie that includes ingredients like bananas, oats, or a spoonful of chia seeds, which are high in prebiotic fiber. Incorporating these foods helps ease your digestive system back into activity, promoting smoother digestion and supporting a healthy gut. By adopting these tips and integrating the following recipes into your diet, you'll create a supportive environment for your gut microbiome that complements your fasting practice.

Breakfast

109. Probiotic Greek Yogurt & Berries Bowl

Description: A creamy bowl of Greek yogurt topped with fresh berries, offering probiotics and antioxidants to support a healthy gut and immune system.

Servings: 1 | **Prep time**: 5 minutes | **Cooking time**: 0 minutes

Ingredients:

➤ 1 cup Greek yogurt (with live cultures)
➤ ½ cup mixed berries (blueberries, strawberries)
➤ 1 tbsp chia seeds
➤ 1 tsp honey (optional)

Preparation Steps: In a bowl, add Greek yogurt and top with mixed berries and chia seeds. Drizzle with honey if desired, and enjoy immediately for a probiotic-rich breakfast.

Ratings: Calories: 200 kcal | Probiotic Support: 5/5 | Antioxidant Power: 5/5 | Digestive Health: 5/5 | Satiety Factor: 4/5 | Energy Boost: 4/5

110. Prebiotic Oats with Chia Seeds

Description: This nourishing bowl of oats with chia seeds is packed with prebiotic fiber to fuel beneficial gut bacteria and promote smooth digestion.

Servings: 1 | **Prep time**: 5 minutes | **Cooking time**: 5 minutes

Ingredients:

➤ ½ cup rolled oats
➤ 1 cup water or almond milk
➤ 1 tbsp chia seeds
➤ ½ banana, sliced (for natural sweetness)

Preparation Steps: Cook oats with water or almond milk over medium heat until creamy. Stir in chia seeds and top with sliced banana for added prebiotic fiber. Serve warm.

Ratings: Calories: 220 kcal | Prebiotic Fiber: 5/5 | Digestive Health: 5/5 | Satiety Factor: 5/5 | Blood Sugar Stability: 4/5 | Energy Boost: 4/5

111. Fermented Sauerkraut & Veggie Scramble

Description: This unique veggie scramble with fermented sauerkraut provides a dose of probiotics and fiber, making it ideal for a gut-friendly start to the day.

Servings: 1 | **Prep time**: 5 minutes | **Cooking time**: 5 minutes

Ingredients:

➢ 2 eggs, whisked
➢ ¼ cup sauerkraut (unpasteurized)
➢ ¼ cup bell pepper, diced
➢ Salt and pepper to taste

Preparation Steps: In a skillet, cook bell pepper over medium heat until tender. Add eggs, cooking until scrambled, then fold in sauerkraut just before serving to retain probiotics. Season with salt and pepper.

Ratings: Calories: 180 kcal | Probiotic Support: 5/5 | Protein Support: 4/5 | Digestive Health: 4/5 | Satiety Factor: 4/5 | Gut Support: 5/5

112. Kefir Smoothie with Banana

Description: A creamy kefir and banana smoothie loaded with probiotics and prebiotic fiber to support digestive health and energy levels.

Servings: 1 | **Prep time**: 5 minutes | **Cooking time**: 0 minutes

Ingredients:

➢ 1 cup kefir (unsweetened)
➢ 1 banana
➢ 1 tbsp flaxseeds

Preparation Steps: Blend kefir, banana, and flaxseeds until smooth. Serve immediately for a refreshing, gut-supportive breakfast.

Ratings: Calories: 230 kcal | Probiotic Support: 5/5 | Prebiotic Fiber: 4/5 | Digestive Health: 5/5 | Energy Boost: 4/5 | Satiety Factor: 4/5

113. Chia Pudding with Blueberries

Description: This simple chia pudding with blueberries provides a rich source of prebiotics and fiber, promoting healthy digestion and gut support.

Servings: 1 | **Prep time**: 5 minutes | **Cooking time**: 0 minutes (overnight soak)

Ingredients:

➢ 3 tbsp chia seeds
➢ 1 cup almond milk
➢ ½ cup blueberries

Preparation Steps: Combine chia seeds and almond milk in a jar, stir, and refrigerate overnight. Top with blueberries in the morning and enjoy.

Ratings: Calories: 180 kcal | Fiber Support: 5/5 | Prebiotic Fiber: 5/5 |

Digestive Health: 5/5 | Antioxidant Power: 4/5 | Blood Sugar Stability: 4/5

114. Gut-Friendly Oatmeal with Seeds

Description: A nourishing oatmeal made with a blend of gut-supportive seeds and prebiotic-rich oats, perfect for a gentle start to the day.

Servings: 1 | **Prep time**: 5 minutes | **Cooking time**: 5 minutes

Ingredients:

➢ ½ cup rolled oats
➢ 1 cup water or milk of choice
➢ 1 tbsp flaxseeds
➢ 1 tbsp sunflower seeds

Preparation Steps: Cook oats with water or milk over medium heat until creamy. Stir in flaxseeds and sunflower seeds and enjoy immediately.

Ratings: Calories: 220 kcal | Prebiotic Fiber: 5/5 | Satiety Factor: 5/5 | Digestive Health: 5/5 | Blood Sugar Stability: 4/5 | Energy Boost: 4/5

115. Ginger & Apple Smoothie

Description: This refreshing smoothie combines ginger and apple for a fiber-rich, gut-friendly drink with anti-inflammatory properties.

Servings: 1 | **Prep time**: 5 minutes | **Cooking time**: 0 minutes

Ingredients:

➢ 1 apple, chopped
➢ 1 tbsp grated ginger
➢ 1 cup coconut water
➢ ½ cup ice cubes

Preparation Steps: Blend apple, ginger, coconut water, and ice until smooth. Serve immediately for a refreshing, gut-friendly boost.

Ratings: Calories: 150 kcal | Anti-Inflammatory Support: 5/5 | Prebiotic Fiber: 4/5 | Digestive Health: 5/5 | Hydration Support: 4/5 | Blood Sugar Stability: 4/5

116. Green Tea & Spinach Smoothie Bowl

Description: A light and refreshing green tea and spinach smoothie bowl, loaded with antioxidants and prebiotics to support gut health.

Servings: 1 | **Prep time**: 5 minutes | **Cooking time**: 0 minutes

Ingredients:

➢ ½ cup brewed green tea, cooled
➢ 1 cup spinach
➢ 1 banana
➢ 1 tbsp chia seeds

Preparation Steps: Blend green tea, spinach, banana, and chia seeds until smooth. Pour into a bowl and enjoy as a smoothie bowl.

Ratings: Calories: 180 kcal | Antioxidant Power: 5/5 | Prebiotic Fiber: 4/5 |

Digestive Health: 5/5 | Blood Sugar Stability: 4/5 | Hydration Support: 4/5

117. Gut-Boosting Berry Protein Bowl

Description: This berry and protein bowl is rich in antioxidants and fiber, promoting gut health and providing a satisfying start to your day.

Servings: 1 | **Prep time**: 5 minutes | **Cooking time**: 0 minutes

Ingredients:

➢ 1 cup Greek yogurt
➢ ½ cup mixed berries
➢ 1 tbsp chia seeds
➢ 1 scoop protein powder (optional)

Preparation Steps: In a bowl, combine Greek yogurt with berries, chia seeds, and protein powder if desired. Stir well and serve.

Ratings: Calories: 220 kcal | Protein Support: 5/5 | Antioxidant Power: 5/5 | Digestive Health: 4/5 | Satiety Factor: 5/5 | Gut Support: 4/5

118. Ginger & Turmeric Breakfast Smoothie

Description: A vibrant smoothie with ginger and turmeric, offering anti-inflammatory benefits and prebiotics for optimal gut health.

Servings: 1 | **Prep time**: 5 minutes | **Cooking time**: 0 minutes

Ingredients:

➢ 1 cup almond milk
➢ 1 tsp grated ginger
➢ ½ tsp turmeric powder
➢ ½ banana

Preparation Steps: Blend almond milk, ginger, turmeric, and banana until smooth. Serve immediately for a refreshing start.

Ratings: Calories: 180 kcal | Anti-Inflammatory Support: 5/5 | Prebiotic Fiber: 4/5 | Digestive Health: 5/5 | Blood Sugar Stability: 4/5 | Hydration Support: 4/5

119. Apple Cider Vinegar & Green Juice

Description: A green juice with apple cider vinegar, packed with prebiotics and cleansing properties, perfect for a refreshing and gut-supportive breakfast drink.

Servings: 1 | **Prep time**: 5 minutes | **Cooking time**: 0 minutes

Ingredients:

➢ 1 cup spinach
➢ 1 green apple, chopped
➢ 1 tbsp apple cider vinegar
➢ 1 cup water
➢ ½ cup ice cubes

Preparation Steps: Blend spinach, green apple, apple cider vinegar, water, and ice until smooth. Serve immediately.

Ratings: Calories: 90 kcal | Prebiotic Fiber: 4/5 | Digestive Health: 5/5 | Blood Sugar Stability: 4/5 | Hydration Support: 5/5 | Cleansing Support: 4/5

120. Lemon & Mint Probiotic Smoothie

Description: A refreshing lemon and mint smoothie with probiotics, designed to support gut health and provide a hydrating start to your day.

Servings: 1 | **Prep time**: 5 minutes | **Cooking time**: 0 minutes

Ingredients:

➢ 1 cup kefir or plain yogurt
➢ 1 tbsp lemon juice
➢ 1 tbsp fresh mint leaves
➢ ½ cup ice cubes

Preparation Steps: Blend kefir or yogurt with lemon juice, mint leaves, and ice until smooth. Serve immediately.

Ratings: Calories: 150 kcal | Probiotic Support: 5/5 | Hydration Support: 5/5 | Digestive Health: 5/5 | Satiety Factor: 4/5 | Blood Sugar Stability: 4/5

Lunch

121. Kimchi & Cabbage Salad with Sesame Dressing

Description: A vibrant salad featuring kimchi and cabbage, packed with probiotics and fiber to support gut health and digestion.

Servings: 2 | **Prep time**: 10 minutes | **Cooking time**: 0 minutes

Ingredients:

➢ 1 cup shredded cabbage
➢ ½ cup kimchi
➢ 1 tbsp sesame seeds
➢ 1 tbsp sesame oil
➢ 1 tbsp rice vinegar

Preparation Steps: In a bowl, mix shredded cabbage and kimchi. Drizzle with sesame oil and rice vinegar, sprinkle with sesame seeds, and toss to combine. Serve immediately.

Ratings: Calories: 180 kcal | Probiotic Support: 5/5 | Fiber Support: 5/5 | Digestive Health: 5/5 | Blood Sugar Stability: 4/5 | Satiety Factor: 4/5

122. Gut-Healthy Miso Soup with Tofu

Description: A soothing miso soup with tofu, rich in probiotics and perfect for supporting gut health with every sip.

Servings: 2 | **Prep time**: 5 minutes | **Cooking time**: 10 minutes

Ingredients:

➢ 3 cups water
➢ 2 tbsp miso paste
➢ ½ cup tofu, cubed
➢ 1 green onion, chopped
➢ 1 tbsp seaweed (optional)

Preparation Steps: In a pot, bring water to a gentle simmer. Add miso paste, stirring until dissolved. Add tofu and cook for a few minutes. Garnish with green onion and seaweed before serving.

Ratings: Calories: 90 kcal | Probiotic Support: 5/5 | Digestive Health: 5/5 | Hydration Support: 5/5 | Satiety Factor: 3/5 | Low-Calorie Option: 5/5

123. Collard Wraps with Avocado & Pickles

Description: These gut-friendly collard wraps are packed with avocado and fermented pickles, providing fiber, healthy fats, and probiotics.

Servings: 2 | **Prep time**: 10 minutes | **Cooking time**: 0 minutes

Ingredients:

➢ 4 large collard green leaves
➢ 1 avocado, sliced
➢ ¼ cup fermented pickles, sliced
➢ 1 tbsp hummus

Preparation Steps: Spread hummus onto each collard leaf, then layer with avocado and pickles. Roll tightly and serve immediately.

Ratings: Calories: 220 kcal | Fiber Support: 5/5 | Probiotic Support: 4/5 | Healthy Fats: 4/5 | Satiety Factor: 4/5 | Blood Sugar Stability: 5/5

124. Lentil Salad with Gut-Boosting Dressing

Description: A protein-packed lentil salad with a gut-supportive dressing, filled with

fiber and nutrients to nourish the digestive system.

Servings: 2 | **Prep time**: 10 minutes | **Cooking time**: 20 minutes

Ingredients:

➢ 1 cup cooked lentils
➢ ½ cup diced cucumber
➢ ¼ cup shredded carrots
➢ 1 tbsp apple cider vinegar
➢ 1 tbsp olive oil

Preparation Steps: Combine lentils, cucumber, and carrots in a bowl. Drizzle with apple cider vinegar and olive oil, toss well, and serve.

Ratings: Calories: 240 kcal | Fiber Support: 5/5 | Prebiotic Fiber: 4/5 | Digestive Health: 5/5 | Satiety Factor: 5/5 | Blood Sugar Stability: 5/5

125. Fermented Pickle & Sprout Wrap

Description: A simple wrap featuring fermented pickles and fresh sprouts, offering a mix of probiotics and fiber for a gut-friendly lunch.

Servings: 1 | **Prep time**: 5 minutes | **Cooking time**: 0 minutes

Ingredients:

➢ 1 large whole-grain wrap
➢ ¼ cup fermented pickles, sliced
➢ ¼ cup sprouts
➢ 1 tbsp hummus

Preparation Steps: Spread hummus on the wrap, layer with pickles and sprouts, and roll tightly. Serve immediately for a quick, gut-boosting meal.

Ratings: Calories: 180 kcal | Probiotic Support: 4/5 | Fiber Support: 4/5 | Digestive Health: 5/5 | Satiety Factor: 4/5 | Blood Sugar Stability: 4/5

126. Microgreens & Sprouts Salad

Description: A light, nutrient-dense salad with microgreens and sprouts, providing fiber, vitamins, and a boost to gut health.

Servings: 2 | **Prep time**: 5 minutes | **Cooking time**: 0 minutes

Ingredients:

- 1 cup microgreens
- 1 cup mixed sprouts
- 1 tbsp olive oil
- 1 tbsp lemon juice

Preparation Steps: In a bowl, combine microgreens and sprouts. Drizzle with olive oil and lemon juice, toss, and serve immediately.

Ratings: Calories: 120 kcal | Fiber Support: 4/5 | Digestive Health: 5/5 | Blood Sugar Stability: 4/5 | Satiety Factor: 3/5 | Antioxidant Power: 5/5

127. Beet & Carrot Gut-Health Bowl

Description: This colorful bowl features beets and carrots, both rich in fiber and prebiotics, ideal for a gut-nourishing lunch.

Servings: 2 | **Prep time**: 10 minutes | **Cooking time**: 5 minutes

Ingredients:

- 1 cup grated beets
- 1 cup shredded carrots
- 1 tbsp apple cider vinegar
- 1 tbsp olive oil

Preparation Steps: Toss grated beets and carrots with apple cider vinegar and olive oil. Serve immediately or let sit briefly for flavors to meld.

Ratings: Calories: 180 kcal | Prebiotic Fiber: 5/5 | Digestive Health: 5/5 | Satiety Factor: 4/5 | Blood Sugar Stability: 4/5 | Antioxidant Power: 4/5

128. Mixed Greens with Avocado & Fermented Veggies

Description: A refreshing salad of mixed greens with avocado and fermented veggies, offering a perfect blend of fiber, healthy fats, and probiotics.

Servings: 2 | **Prep time**: 5 minutes | **Cooking time**: 0 minutes

Ingredients:

- 2 cups mixed greens
- 1 avocado, sliced
- ¼ cup fermented vegetables (e.g., sauerkraut or kimchi)
- 1 tbsp olive oil

Preparation Steps: In a large bowl, combine mixed greens, avocado slices, and fermented vegetables. Drizzle with olive oil and toss gently before serving.

Ratings: Calories: 220 kcal | Probiotic Support: 5/5 | Fiber Support: 5/5 | Healthy Fats: 4/5 | Digestive Health: 5/5 | Satiety Factor: 5/5

129. Probiotic Chicken Salad with Yogurt

Description: A creamy chicken salad made with probiotic-rich yogurt, providing a protein-packed, gut-friendly lunch.

Servings: 2 | **Prep time**: 10 minutes | **Cooking time**: 0 minutes

Ingredients:

➢ 1 cup cooked chicken breast, diced
➢ ¼ cup Greek yogurt (with live cultures)
➢ 1 tbsp fresh dill, chopped
➢ 1 celery stalk, diced

Preparation Steps: In a bowl, mix chicken, Greek yogurt, dill, and celery until well combined. Serve on its own or over a bed of greens.

Ratings: Calories: 250 kcal | Protein Support: 5/5 | Probiotic Support: 5/5 | Digestive Health: 4/5 | Satiety Factor: 5/5 | Blood Sugar Stability: 5/5

130. Sautéed Mushrooms & Greens Salad

Description: A warm salad with sautéed mushrooms and mixed greens, offering

fiber, vitamins, and prebiotic benefits for gut health.

Servings: 2 | **Prep time**: 5 minutes | **Cooking time**: 10 minutes

Ingredients:

➢ 1 cup mushrooms, sliced
➢ 2 cups mixed greens
➢ 1 tbsp olive oil
➢ Salt and pepper to taste

Preparation Steps: Sauté mushrooms in olive oil over medium heat until golden. Toss with mixed greens, season with salt and pepper, and serve warm.

Ratings: Calories: 180 kcal | Prebiotic Fiber: 4/5 | Digestive Health: 5/5 | Satiety Factor: 4/5 | Blood Sugar Stability: 4/5 | Antioxidant Power: 4/5

Dinner

131. Probiotic-Rich Salmon with Sauerkraut

Description: A nutrient-packed dinner featuring grilled salmon and probiotic-rich sauerkraut, ideal for supporting digestion and gut health.

Servings: 2 | **Prep time**: 5 minutes | **Cooking time**: 10 minutes

Ingredients:

➢ 2 salmon fillets
➢ ½ cup sauerkraut (unpasteurized)
➢ 1 tbsp olive oil
➢ Salt and pepper to taste

Preparation Steps: Season salmon with salt and pepper. Grill over medium heat for about 5 minutes per side until cooked through. Serve with sauerkraut on the side for a gut-friendly meal.

Ratings: Calories: 320 kcal | Probiotic Support: 5/5 | Omega-3 Support: 5/5 | Digestive Health: 5/5 | Protein Support: 5/5 | Satiety Factor: 4/5

132. Roasted Root Vegetable Soup with Bone Broth

Description: A comforting, gut-healing soup made with roasted root vegetables and bone broth, providing essential nutrients and collagen for digestive health.

Servings: 2 | **Prep time**: 10 minutes | **Cooking time**: 30 minutes

Ingredients:

➢ 1 cup diced carrots
➢ 1 cup diced sweet potatoes
➢ 2 cups bone broth
➢ 1 tbsp olive oil
➢ Salt and pepper to taste

Preparation Steps: Toss carrots and sweet potatoes with olive oil, salt, and pepper, and roast at 400°F (200°C) for 20 minutes. Transfer to a pot, add bone broth, and simmer for 10 minutes. Serve warm.

Ratings: Calories: 280 kcal | Collagen Support: 5/5 | Digestive Health: 5/5 | Satiety Factor: 4/5 | Blood Sugar Stability: 4/5 | Anti-Inflammatory Support: 4/5

133. Baked Miso Cod with Bok Choy

Description: A flavorful baked miso cod served with bok choy, rich in probiotics and essential nutrients to support gut health.

Servings: 2 | **Prep time**: 10 minutes | **Cooking time**: 15 minutes

Ingredients:

➢ 2 cod fillets
➢ 1 tbsp miso paste
➢ 2 cups bok choy, halved
➢ 1 tbsp sesame oil

Preparation Steps: Preheat oven to 375°F (190°C). Spread miso paste on cod fillets. Place cod and bok choy on a baking sheet, drizzle with sesame oil, and bake for 15 minutes until cod is flaky and bok choy is tender.

Ratings: Calories: 250 kcal | Probiotic Support: 4/5 | Fiber Support: 4/5 | Digestive Health: 5/5 | Blood Sugar Stability: 4/5 | Satiety Factor: 4/5

134. Roasted Garlic & Veggie Broth Soup

Description: A soothing veggie broth with roasted garlic and vegetables, offering prebiotic fiber and hydration to support gut health.

Servings: 2 | **Prep time**: 10 minutes | **Cooking time**: 20 minutes

Ingredients:

➢ 3 cups vegetable broth
➢ 1 head of garlic, roasted

> 1 cup mixed vegetables (e.g., carrots, celery)
> Salt and pepper to taste

Preparation Steps: Squeeze roasted garlic into vegetable broth, add mixed vegetables, and simmer for 20 minutes. Serve hot for a comforting, gut-nourishing meal.

Ratings: Calories: 120 kcal | Prebiotic Fiber: 4/5 | Digestive Health: 5/5 | Satiety Factor: 3/5 | Hydration Support: 5/5 | Blood Sugar Stability: 4/5

135. Ginger & Carrot Stir Fry with Chicken

Description: A light stir-fry with ginger, carrots, and lean chicken, providing protein, anti-inflammatory benefits, and fiber for gut health.

Servings: 2 | **Prep time**: 5 minutes | **Cooking time**: 10 minutes

Ingredients:

> 1 cup chicken breast, sliced
> 1 cup carrots, julienned
> 1 tbsp grated ginger
> 1 tbsp olive oil
> Salt and pepper to taste

Preparation Steps: Heat olive oil in a skillet over medium heat. Add ginger, chicken, and carrots, cooking until chicken is cooked through. Season with salt and pepper, and serve.

Ratings: Calories: 220 kcal | Protein Support: 5/5 | Anti-Inflammatory Support: 5/5 | Digestive Health: 4/5 | Satiety Factor: 4/5 | Blood Sugar Stability: 4/5

136. Sauerkraut & Herb Salad with Grilled Fish

Description: A fresh herb salad paired with grilled fish and sauerkraut, offering a blend of probiotics and omega-3s to support gut and heart health.

Servings: 2 | **Prep time**: 5 minutes | **Cooking time**: 10 minutes

Ingredients:

> 2 white fish fillets (e.g., tilapia or cod)
> ½ cup sauerkraut
> 1 cup mixed herbs (e.g., parsley, cilantro)
> 1 tbsp olive oil

Preparation Steps: Grill fish fillets for 5 minutes per side. Serve with mixed herbs and sauerkraut on the side for a refreshing, probiotic-rich meal.

Ratings: Calories: 230 kcal | Probiotic Support: 5/5 | Omega-3 Support: 4/5 | Digestive Health: 5/5 | Satiety Factor: 4/5 | Blood Sugar Stability: 5/5

137. Turmeric-Spiced Lentil Soup

Description: A warm and hearty lentil soup spiced with turmeric, packed with fiber, protein, and anti-inflammatory benefits for a gut-friendly dinner.

Servings: 2 | **Prep time**: 10 minutes | **Cooking time**: 25 minutes

Ingredients:

➤ 1 cup lentils, rinsed

➤ 3 cups vegetable broth

➤ 1 tsp turmeric powder

➤ Salt and pepper to taste

Preparation Steps: In a pot, combine lentils, vegetable broth, and turmeric. Simmer for 25 minutes until lentils are tender. Season with salt and pepper and serve warm.

Ratings: Calories: 250 kcal | Anti-Inflammatory Support: 5/5 | Fiber Support: 5/5 | Digestive Health: 5/5 | Satiety Factor: 5/5 | Blood Sugar Stability: 4/5

138. Gut-Healing Roasted Squash & Broccoli

Description: A simple yet nourishing dinner of roasted squash and broccoli, both rich in fiber and vitamins to support gut health.

Servings: 2 | **Prep time**: 5 minutes | **Cooking time**: 20 minutes

Ingredients:

➤ 1 cup butternut squash, cubed

➤ 1 cup broccoli florets

➤ 1 tbsp olive oil

➤ Salt and pepper to taste

Preparation Steps: Toss butternut squash and broccoli with olive oil, salt, and pepper. Roast at 400°F (200°C) for 20 minutes until tender.

Ratings: Calories: 180 kcal | Fiber Support: 5/5 | Digestive Health: 5/5 |

Antioxidant Power: 4/5 | Blood Sugar Stability: 4/5 | Satiety Factor: 4/5

139. Fermented Kimchi Veggie Stir Fry

Description: A vibrant stir fry featuring fermented kimchi and vegetables, offering probiotics and prebiotics to nourish the gut.

Servings: 2 | **Prep time**: 5 minutes | **Cooking time**: 10 minutes

Ingredients:

➤ ½ cup kimchi

➤ 1 cup mixed vegetables (e.g., bell peppers, carrots, zucchini)

➤ 1 tbsp sesame oil

➤ 1 tsp soy sauce

Preparation Steps: Heat sesame oil in a skillet, add mixed vegetables, and stir-fry until tender. Add kimchi and soy sauce, stirring until combined. Serve warm.

Ratings: Calories: 150 kcal | Probiotic Support: 5/5 | Fiber Support: 4/5 | Digestive Health: 5/5 | Blood Sugar Stability: 4/5 | Satiety Factor: 3/5

140. Miso-Glazed Salmon with Greens

Description: A delicious miso-glazed salmon served with mixed greens, offering a blend of probiotics, omega-3s, and fiber to support gut health.

Servings: 2 | **Prep time**: 10 minutes | **Cooking time**: 10 minutes

Ingredients:

- ➤ 2 salmon fillets
- ➤ 1 tbsp miso paste
- ➤ 2 cups mixed greens
- ➤ 1 tbsp olive oil

Preparation Steps: Spread miso paste on salmon fillets. Heat olive oil in a skillet, add salmon, and cook for 5 minutes on each side. Serve with mixed greens for a refreshing, gut-friendly meal.

Ratings: Calories: 300 kcal | Probiotic Support: 4/5 | Omega-3 Support: 5/5 | Digestive Health: 5/5 | Satiety Factor: 5/5 | Blood Sugar Stability: 5/5

Chapter 5: Anti-Inflammatory Recipes for Joint and Skin Health

Chronic inflammation can impact not only your joints and skin but also your overall wellness. By focusing on anti-inflammatory foods, you can support your body's natural defenses against inflammation, leading to improved joint function, radiant skin, and enhanced vitality. This chapter is dedicated to recipes rich in antioxidants, omega-3s, vitamins, and minerals that help reduce inflammation and boost health from the inside out.

In addition to these recipes, you'll find helpful tips for incorporating anti-inflammatory foods into your daily diet and utilizing fasting to manage inflammation. Fasting, when paired with anti-inflammatory foods, can create an environment that naturally reduces inflammation and promotes cellular repair, allowing you to feel and look your best.

Anti-Inflammatory Fasting Tips

Managing Inflammation with Fasting

Fasting can be a powerful tool for managing inflammation, especially when combined with a diet rich in anti-inflammatory foods. During fasting periods, the body enters a repair state where it removes damaged cells and reduces inflammation. By reducing meal frequency, fasting gives the body a break from continuous digestion, allowing it to focus on cellular repair processes. Intermittent fasting schedules, like the 16:8 method, can be particularly beneficial, as they give your digestive system time to rest and support reduced inflammation without overly restricting nutrient intake.

It's essential, however, to approach fasting with balance. Long fasting periods should be broken with gentle, anti-inflammatory foods like leafy greens, berries, and omega-3-rich foods. This approach helps reduce oxidative stress and inflammation, allowing you to experience the benefits of fasting without compromising your body's need for nutrients.

Incorporating Anti-Inflammatory Foods into Your Diet

An anti-inflammatory diet emphasizes foods rich in antioxidants, omega-3 fatty acids, and fiber. Key ingredients to focus on include fatty fish, leafy greens, berries, turmeric, ginger, nuts, and seeds, all of which are scientifically linked to reduced inflammation. Incorporating these foods into every meal—especially around your fasting periods—can help maintain low inflammation levels in the body.

For example, breaking a fast with a turmeric and ginger smoothie or a leafy green salad with salmon allows you to introduce nutrients that support the body's anti-inflammatory processes. Another simple approach is to add a teaspoon of turmeric or a dash of cinnamon to your morning smoothie, both of which have strong anti-inflammatory properties. By regularly consuming anti-inflammatory foods, you'll improve joint and skin health, boost immunity, and feel more balanced and resilient.

These following recipes provide easy, flavorful options that bring anti-inflammatory ingredients into your daily meals, supporting both joint health and skin vitality.

Breakfast

141. Anti-Inflammatory Golden Milk Smoothie

Description: A creamy, anti-inflammatory smoothie featuring turmeric, ginger, and almond milk, perfect for a warming start that supports joint and skin health.

Servings: 1 | **Prep time**: 5 minutes | **Cooking time**: 0 minutes

Ingredients:

➢ 1 cup almond milk
➢ 1 tsp turmeric powder
➢ ½ tsp ginger powder
➢ 1 banana
➢ 1 tsp honey (optional)

Preparation Steps: Blend almond milk, turmeric, ginger, and banana until smooth. Serve immediately for a creamy, nutrient-packed breakfast.

Ratings: Calories: 180 kcal | Anti-Inflammatory Support: 5/5 | Skin Vitality: 4/5 | Digestive Health: 4/5 | Satiety Factor: 4/5 | Energy Boost: 4/5

142. Turmeric & Cinnamon Yogurt Bowl

Description: This yogurt bowl combines turmeric and cinnamon with Greek yogurt, offering anti-inflammatory properties and probiotics for a balanced start to your day.

Servings: 1 | **Prep time**: 5 minutes | **Cooking time**: 0 minutes

Ingredients:

➢ 1 cup Greek yogurt
➢ ½ tsp turmeric powder
➢ ½ tsp cinnamon
➢ 1 tbsp chia seeds
➢ ¼ cup blueberries

Preparation Steps: In a bowl, mix Greek yogurt with turmeric and cinnamon. Top with chia seeds and blueberries, and enjoy immediately.

Ratings: Calories: 200 kcal | Anti-Inflammatory Support: 5/5 | Probiotic Support: 4/5 | Skin Vitality: 4/5 | Satiety Factor: 5/5 | Blood Sugar Stability: 4/5

143. Pumpkin & Chia Seed Porridge

Description: A cozy pumpkin porridge rich in beta-carotene and omega-3s, offering anti-inflammatory benefits and nutrients for skin health.

Servings: 1 | **Prep time**: 5 minutes | **Cooking time**: 5 minutes

Ingredients:

- ½ cup canned pumpkin puree
- ½ cup almond milk
- 1 tbsp chia seeds
- ½ tsp cinnamon
- 1 tsp maple syrup (optional)

Preparation Steps: In a pot, heat pumpkin puree and almond milk over medium heat. Stir in chia seeds and cinnamon, and cook until warmed through. Drizzle with maple syrup if desired and serve.

Ratings: Calories: 180 kcal | Anti-Inflammatory Support: 4/5 | Fiber Support: 5/5 | Skin Vitality: 5/5 | Blood Sugar Stability: 4/5 | Satiety Factor: 4/5

144. Beet & Berry Smoothie

Description: A vibrant smoothie made with beets and berries, rich in antioxidants and anti-inflammatory compounds that support joint and skin health.

Servings: 1 | **Prep time:** 5 minutes | **Cooking time:** 0 minutes

Ingredients:

- ½ cup cooked beetroot, diced
- ½ cup mixed berries
- 1 cup coconut water
- 1 tbsp chia seeds

Preparation Steps: Blend beetroot, berries, coconut water, and chia seeds until smooth. Serve immediately for a refreshing, gut-supportive breakfast.

Ratings: Calories: 160 kcal | Anti-Inflammatory Support: 5/5 | Antioxidant Power: 5/5 | Skin Vitality: 5/5 | Blood Sugar Stability: 4/5 | Hydration Support: 4/5

145. Anti-Inflammatory Green Smoothie Bowl

Description: A nourishing green smoothie bowl with anti-inflammatory ingredients like spinach, ginger, and flaxseeds to boost joint health and skin resilience.

Servings: 1 | **Prep time:** 5 minutes | **Cooking time:** 0 minutes

Ingredients:

- 1 cup spinach
- 1 banana
- ½ tsp ginger powder
- 1 tbsp flaxseeds
- ½ cup almond milk

Preparation Steps: Blend spinach, banana, ginger, flaxseeds, and almond milk until smooth. Pour into a bowl and enjoy with your favorite toppings.

Ratings: Calories: 190 kcal | Anti-Inflammatory Support: 5/5 | Skin Vitality: 4/5 | Digestive Health: 5/5 | Satiety Factor: 4/5 | Blood Sugar Stability: 4/5

Lunch

146. Anti-Inflammatory Carrot Ginger Soup

Description: A warm and soothing carrot ginger soup that's packed with anti-inflammatory ingredients, supporting joint health and boosting skin vitality.

Servings: 2 | **Prep time**: 10 minutes | **Cooking time**: 20 minutes

Ingredients:

- 3 large carrots, chopped
- 1 tbsp fresh ginger, grated
- 2 cups vegetable broth
- 1 tbsp olive oil
- Salt and pepper to taste

Preparation Steps: In a pot, heat olive oil over medium heat, add carrots and ginger, and sauté for a few minutes. Pour in vegetable broth, bring to a boil, and simmer until carrots are tender. Blend until smooth and season with salt and pepper.

Ratings: Calories: 180 kcal | Anti-Inflammatory Support: 5/5 | Digestive Health: 4/5 | Skin Vitality: 4/5 | Blood Sugar Stability: 4/5 | Hydration Support: 4/5

147. Spinach & Walnut Salad with Balsamic

Description: A simple spinach salad with crunchy walnuts and a balsamic drizzle, providing omega-3s and antioxidants to reduce inflammation and support skin health.

Servings: 2 | **Prep time**: 5 minutes | **Cooking time**: 0 minutes

Ingredients:

- 2 cups spinach

- ¼ cup walnuts, chopped
- 1 tbsp balsamic vinegar
- 1 tbsp olive oil

Preparation Steps: In a bowl, combine spinach and walnuts. Drizzle with balsamic vinegar and olive oil, toss well, and serve immediately.

Ratings: Calories: 220 kcal | Anti-Inflammatory Support: 4/5 | Omega-3 Support: 5/5 | Skin Vitality: 5/5 | Digestive Health: 4/5 | Blood Sugar Stability: 4/5

148. Salmon Salad with Avocado & Herbs

Description: A nourishing salmon and avocado salad with fresh herbs, packed with anti-inflammatory omega-3s to support joint and skin health.

Servings: 2 | **Prep time**: 10 minutes | **Cooking time**: 0 minutes

Ingredients:

- 1 cup cooked salmon, flaked
- 1 avocado, diced
- 1 tbsp fresh dill, chopped
- 1 tbsp lemon juice
- Salt and pepper to taste

Preparation Steps: In a bowl, mix flaked salmon, diced avocado, and dill. Drizzle with lemon juice, season with salt and pepper, and serve immediately.

Ratings: Calories: 300 kcal | Omega-3 Support: 5/5 | Healthy Fats: 5/5 | Anti-Inflammatory Support: 5/5 | Satiety Factor: 5/5 | Skin Vitality: 5/5

149. Sweet Potato & Kale Salad

Description: A hearty salad with roasted sweet potatoes and fresh kale, rich in beta-carotene and antioxidants to combat inflammation and support skin health.

Servings: 2 | **Prep time**: 10 minutes | **Cooking time**: 20 minutes

Ingredients:

➢ 1 cup sweet potato, cubed and roasted
➢ 2 cups kale, chopped
➢ 1 tbsp olive oil
➢ 1 tbsp apple cider vinegar
➢ Salt and pepper to taste

Preparation Steps: In a large bowl, massage kale with olive oil and apple cider vinegar. Add roasted sweet potato cubes, season with salt and pepper, and toss well.

Ratings: Calories: 240 kcal | Anti-Inflammatory Support: 4/5 | Fiber Support: 5/5 | Skin Vitality: 4/5 | Satiety Factor: 4/5 | Digestive Health: 4/5

150. Zucchini & Olive Salad

Description: A light and flavorful zucchini and olive salad, rich in antioxidants and healthy fats to reduce inflammation and support joint health.

Servings: 2 | **Prep time**: 5 minutes | **Cooking time**: 0 minutes

Ingredients:

➢ 1 large zucchini, spiralized or thinly sliced
➢ ¼ cup black olives, sliced
➢ 1 tbsp olive oil
➢ 1 tbsp lemon juice
➢ Salt and pepper to taste

Preparation Steps: In a bowl, combine spiralized zucchini and olives. Drizzle with olive oil and lemon juice, season with salt and pepper, and toss to combine. Serve fresh.

Ratings: Calories: 180 kcal | Anti-Inflammatory Support: 4/5 | Healthy Fats: 4/5 | Skin Vitality: 4/5 | Digestive Health: 4/5 | Blood Sugar Stability: 4/5

Dinner

151. Golden Cauliflower & Chickpea Curry

Description: A warming, golden curry with anti-inflammatory turmeric and fiber-rich chickpeas, perfect for a satisfying, joint-supportive dinner.

Servings: 2 | **Prep time**: 10 minutes | **Cooking time**: 25 minutes

Ingredients:

➢ 1 cup cauliflower florets
➢ 1 cup chickpeas, rinsed and drained
➢ 1 cup coconut milk
➢ 1 tbsp turmeric powder
➢ 1 tsp cumin
➢ Salt and pepper to taste

Preparation Steps: In a pot, combine coconut milk, turmeric, cumin, cauliflower, and chickpeas. Simmer over medium heat for 20-25 minutes until cauliflower is tender. Season with salt and pepper, and serve warm.

Ratings: Calories: 300 kcal | Anti-Inflammatory Support: 5/5 | Fiber Support: 5/5 | Digestive Health: 4/5 | Satiety Factor: 5/5 | Skin Vitality: 4/5

152. Baked Salmon with Turmeric & Lemon

Description: A simple and flavorful baked salmon with turmeric and lemon, packed with omega-3s and antioxidants for joint and skin health.

Servings: 2 | **Prep time**: 5 minutes | **Cooking time**: 15 minutes

Ingredients:

➢ 2 salmon fillets
➢ 1 tsp turmeric powder
➢ 1 tbsp lemon juice
➢ 1 tbsp olive oil
➢ Salt and pepper to taste

Preparation Steps: Preheat oven to 375°F (190°C). Rub salmon with turmeric, lemon juice, and olive oil. Place on a baking sheet, season with salt and pepper, and bake for 15 minutes until cooked through.

Ratings: Calories: 320 kcal | Omega-3 Support: 5/5 | Anti-Inflammatory Support: 5/5 | Skin Vitality: 5/5 | Satiety Factor: 5/5 | Blood Sugar Stability: 4/5

153. Ginger & Garlic Shrimp

Description: A quick and anti-inflammatory dish featuring shrimp cooked with fresh ginger and garlic, supporting joint health and digestion.

Servings: 2 | **Prep time**: 5 minutes | **Cooking time**: 10 minutes

Ingredients:

➢ 1 cup shrimp, peeled and deveined
➢ 1 tbsp fresh ginger, grated
➢ 2 cloves garlic, minced
➢ 1 tbsp olive oil
➢ Salt and pepper to taste

Preparation Steps: Heat olive oil in a skillet over medium heat. Add ginger and garlic, cook for a minute, then add shrimp. Sauté until shrimp are pink and cooked through. Season with salt and pepper.

Ratings: Calories: 180 kcal | Anti-Inflammatory Support: 5/5 | Protein Support: 4/5 | Digestive Health: 4/5 | Skin Vitality: 4/5 | Blood Sugar Stability: 4/5

154. Sautéed Greens with Roasted Sweet Potatoes

Description: A hearty dinner of sautéed greens and roasted sweet potatoes, rich in beta-carotene and antioxidants for anti-inflammatory support.

Servings: 2 | **Prep time**: 10 minutes | **Cooking time**: 20 minutes

Ingredients:

➢ 2 cups mixed greens (e.g., spinach, kale)
➢ 1 cup sweet potatoes, cubed

➢ 1 tbsp olive oil
➢ Salt and pepper to taste

Preparation Steps: Roast sweet potatoes at 400°F (200°C) for 20 minutes until tender. Meanwhile, sauté greens in olive oil until wilted. Combine and season with salt and pepper.

Ratings: Calories: 220 kcal | Fiber Support: 5/5 | Anti-Inflammatory Support: 4/5 | Skin Vitality: 4/5 | Satiety Factor: 4/5 | Digestive Health: 4/5

155. Anti-Inflammatory Stuffed Bell Peppers with Rice

Description: Colorful bell peppers stuffed with anti-inflammatory spices and rice, offering a satisfying, nutrient-dense meal that supports joint and skin health.

Servings: 2 | **Prep time**: 10 minutes | **Cooking time**: 30 minutes

Ingredients:

➢ 2 large bell peppers, tops removed and seeds scooped out
➢ 1 cup cooked rice
➢ 1 tsp turmeric powder
➢ 1 tsp cumin
➢ Salt and pepper to taste

Preparation Steps: Preheat oven to 375°F (190°C). In a bowl, mix rice with turmeric, cumin, salt, and pepper. Stuff bell peppers with the mixture, place in a baking dish, and bake for 30 minutes until peppers are tender.

Ratings: Calories: 250 kcal | Anti-Inflammatory Support: 5/5 | Fiber Support: 4/5 | Satiety Factor: 5/5 | Digestive Health: 4/5 | Skin Vitality: 4/5

Appendix

Ingredient Index

This index provides a quick reference guide to the key ingredients used throughout the recipes in this cookbook, helping you locate recipes based on specific ingredients. Each ingredient listed here contributes unique health benefits, from anti-inflammatory properties to probiotics and essential nutrients for overall wellness. Use this index to explore recipes that feature your favorite ingredients or to find meals that meet specific dietary goals.

A

- **Almond Milk**: Golden Milk Smoothie (Recipe 141), Anti-Inflammatory Green Smoothie Bowl (Recipe 145)
- **Apple Cider Vinegar**: Beet & Carrot Gut-Health Bowl (Recipe 127), Zucchini & Olive Salad (Recipe 150)
- **Avocado**: Salmon Salad with Avocado & Herbs (Recipe 148), Mixed Greens with Avocado & Fermented Veggies (Recipe 128)

B

- **Banana**: Kefir Smoothie with Banana (Recipe 112), Beet & Berry Smoothie (Recipe 144), Anti-Inflammatory Green Smoothie Bowl (Recipe 145)
- **Basil**: Zucchini & Olive Salad (Recipe 150)

Berries (Mixed)

- **Berries**: Probiotic Greek Yogurt & Berries Bowl (Recipe 109), Beet & Berry Smoothie (Recipe 144), Gut-Boosting Berry Protein Bowl (Recipe 117)

C

- **Cauliflower**: Golden Cauliflower & Chickpea Curry (Recipe 151), Low-Carb Cauliflower & Cheese Frittata (Recipe 78)
- **Carrots**: Anti-Inflammatory Carrot Ginger Soup (Recipe 146), Ginger & Carrot Stir Fry with Chicken (Recipe 135)
- **Chia Seeds**: Probiotic Greek Yogurt & Berries Bowl (Recipe 109), Chia Pudding with Blueberries (Recipe 113), Gut-Friendly Oatmeal with Seeds (Recipe 114)

F

- **Flaxseeds**: Anti-Inflammatory Green Smoothie Bowl (Recipe 145), Coconut & Flax Oatmeal (Recipe 85)

G

- **Ginger**: Ginger & Apple Smoothie (Recipe 115), Anti-

This index allows you to quickly find recipes that feature each ingredient, making it easy to incorporate these health-boosting foods into your meal plan. Whether you're looking for a specific flavor, nutrient, or health benefit, the Ingredient Index will guide you to the perfect recipes.

Quick Reference Guide to Fasting & Gut Health

Fasting is a powerful tool that can give your digestive system a much-needed break, allowing it to rest, reset, and repair. When you pair fasting with a diet that prioritizes gut-friendly foods, the result can be a healthier, more resilient digestive system and improved overall wellness. This guide provides practical insights into the fasting-gut health connection and offers strategies to support your journey.

Understanding the Connection Between Fasting and Gut Health

Fasting provides the body with extended periods away from digestion, allowing energy to be redirected toward cellular repair and renewal. This process supports your digestive system, enabling it to repair itself and restore balance to the gut microbiome. However, a structured approach to both your fasting periods and eating windows is essential to optimize these benefits for gut health.

Key Principles for Enhancing Gut Health During Fasting

To support your gut during fasting, emphasize both prebiotic and probiotic foods. Prebiotics, such as garlic, onions, asparagus, and bananas, feed the beneficial bacteria in your gut, while probiotics, found in yogurt, kefir, kimchi, and sauerkraut, help replenish and balance these bacteria. Together, these foods create a favorable environment for healthy gut flora, supporting digestive resilience and overall balance.

When breaking a fast, it's best to start gently with easily digestible foods. Introducing a small portion of probiotics, like a spoonful of yogurt or kefir, prepares the digestive system for further activity. Following this with prebiotic-rich foods provides fuel for gut bacteria, ensuring the microbiome remains balanced and resilient.

Hydration plays a crucial role in maintaining gut health, especially during fasting periods. Water, herbal teas, or electrolyte-rich fluids keep your digestive system hydrated, reducing the risk of discomfort and allowing for smoother digestion when you return to eating.

Recommended Fasting Schedules to Support Gut Health

The 16:8 intermittent fasting method, where you fast for 16 hours and eat within an 8-hour window, is particularly helpful for gut health. This schedule provides a regular break for your digestive system, fostering a balanced and thriving microbiome. When breaking a 16-hour fast, try starting with gut-supportive foods like a smoothie with chia seeds, bananas, and kefir to introduce probiotics and fiber.

A 24-hour fast once a week can provide deeper rest and repair for your gut. When breaking a 24-hour fast, ease your digestive system back into activity with gentle, probiotic-rich options, like a gut-friendly broth or a miso-based soup. Follow this with a balanced meal that's high in fiber to nourish your microbiome.

Gut Health Strategies During Fasting

During eating windows, incorporating fermented foods like kimchi, sauerkraut, and miso can significantly benefit gut health by providing natural probiotics. These foods can be easily added to salads, soups, or grain bowls, enhancing your gut microbiome with beneficial bacteria.

Fiber-rich foods are also essential during eating windows, as fiber acts as a prebiotic, feeding gut bacteria and promoting regular digestion. High-fiber options like leafy greens, chia seeds, oats, and lentils can help stabilize blood sugar levels and reduce cravings, making fasting periods easier to manage.

Anti-inflammatory foods are particularly beneficial during fasting as they help counteract any temporary inflammation from fasting itself. Including turmeric, ginger, berries, leafy greens, and salmon in your meals supports gut health and reduces inflammation, enhancing your digestive system's resilience.

Fasting-Friendly Meal Suggestions

Breaking a fast gently can help optimize digestion. Starting with a small smoothie that includes kefir, banana, and spinach provides probiotics and fiber to ease your system into digestion. Alternatively, a spoonful of Greek yogurt with chia seeds and berries offers a simple way to introduce probiotics and prebiotics after fasting.

For lunch, a gut-boosting salad with mixed greens, avocado, fermented vegetables, and roasted chickpeas provides fiber and probiotics. At dinner, consider options like a turmeric-spiced lentil soup with sautéed greens. These meals are designed to provide anti-inflammatory support and essential nutrients for digestion and overall wellness.

Foods to Include and Avoid for Optimal Gut Health

For optimal gut health, include a variety of prebiotics and probiotics in your diet. Prebiotics such as garlic, onions, asparagus, apples, and bananas help fuel beneficial bacteria. Probiotic-rich foods like yogurt, kefir, sauerkraut, kimchi, and miso replenish the microbiome. High-fiber foods, including lentils, oats, leafy greens, chia seeds, and flaxseeds, support digestion and maintain balanced blood sugar levels. Anti-inflammatory foods like salmon, berries, ginger, and turmeric further support gut health by reducing inflammation.

On the other hand, refined sugars and highly processed foods can disrupt the gut microbiome, making it important to minimize their intake. Artificial sweeteners such as aspartame and sucralose can also harm beneficial gut bacteria, so it's best to choose natural sweeteners in moderation.

Key Takeaways

By giving your digestive system a break through fasting, you can enhance gut health and microbiome balance. Breaking your fast with gentle, gut-friendly foods optimizes digestion and nutrient absorption. Including a consistent variety of prebiotic, probiotic, and fiber-rich foods in your eating windows will strengthen gut health, making fasting more effective and beneficial for your overall wellness journey.

Additional Resources for Women's Health

Expanding your knowledge on women's health can empower you to make informed decisions and enhance your wellness journey. Below is a collection of valuable resources, from books to websites and podcasts, that cover a wide range of topics related to hormone balance, gut health, fasting, and overall women's wellness. These resources offer both in-depth and practical insights, helping you build a well-rounded approach to your health.

Recommended Books

➢ **"The Hormone Cure" by Dr. Sara Gottfried**
Dr. Gottfried's book delves into the complexities of hormonal imbalances in women, offering actionable insights and lifestyle changes to restore balance. It's a valuable guide for understanding how hormones affect everything from mood to metabolism.

➢ **"Fast Like a Girl" by Dr. Mindy Pelz**
This book focuses on the science behind fasting for women, specifically tailored to hormonal cycles and unique health needs. Dr. Pelz shares practical tips and fasting techniques designed for women of various life stages.

➢ **"The Microbiome Solution" by Dr. Robynne Chutkan**
This resource highlights the essential role of the gut microbiome in women's health, emphasizing diet and lifestyle choices to foster a healthy gut and enhance immune function, mood, and energy.

➢ **"Beyond the Pill" by Dr. Jolene Brighten**
Dr. Brighten offers insights into managing hormonal health beyond contraceptives, providing a comprehensive look at how women can regain hormonal balance through nutrition, lifestyle, and supplement strategies.

Informative Websites

➤ **Office on Women's Health (womenshealth.gov)**
A government resource providing comprehensive information on women's health issues, including menopause, hormone health, and preventive care. This site includes resources on maintaining wellness across all stages of life.

➤ **National Institute of Environmental Health Sciences (niehs.nih.gov)**
This site offers research and resources related to endocrine health, explaining the influence of environmental factors on hormonal balance and overall health.

➤ **MindBodyGreen (mindbodygreen.com)**
With articles on topics such as hormone health, gut wellness, and functional nutrition, MindBodyGreen serves as a trusted platform for women seeking a holistic approach to their health.

Podcasts for Women's Wellness

➤ **"The Goop Podcast"**
This podcast covers a wide variety of health topics, featuring experts on hormonal health, gut health, and integrative wellness practices. It's an accessible way to gain insights on improving well-being through holistic approaches.

➤ **"Well-Fed Women"**
A women-centered podcast hosted by nutrition and wellness experts. This show delves into topics like hormone health, metabolism, and self-care, offering practical advice rooted in scientific knowledge.

➤ **"The Model Health Show" with Shawn Stevenson**
This podcast provides clear, research-based discussions on health topics that matter to women, from fasting and nutrition to mental wellness. Shawn Stevenson's interviews with experts offer actionable insights for optimizing health.

Online Courses and Supportive Communities

➤ **Institute for Integrative Nutrition (integrativenutrition.com)**
Offering online courses in holistic health, this institute provides in-depth training on nutrition, wellness, and hormone health. Courses are beneficial for those interested in a

deeper dive into health education.

➤ **Dr. Mindy Pelz's Community (drmindypelz.com)**
Dr. Pelz offers an online community dedicated to women interested in fasting and hormone health. Her programs provide structured fasting guidance and support from a community of like-minded individuals.

➤ **Hormone Health Network (hormone.org)**
A digital resource dedicated to hormone education, providing tools and information for women seeking to understand and manage their hormonal health. This network connects users to hormone-related resources, patient education, and the latest research in endocrinology.

Recommended Apps for Wellness Tracking

➤ **Clue**
Clue is a user-friendly app for tracking menstrual cycles, moods, and symptoms. It helps women understand how their cycles may impact energy, mood, and dietary needs, making it useful for aligning wellness practices with hormonal patterns.

➤ **MyFitnessPal**
This app is ideal for tracking nutrition and fasting periods, offering customizable tracking tools for women focused on balanced diets and intermittent fasting routines.

➤ **Insight Timer**
Insight Timer provides guided meditations and mindfulness exercises, supporting stress reduction and mental well-being, which are essential for hormone and gut health.

These resources are designed to support you at every step of your wellness journey, offering expert guidance and practical tools for achieving a balanced, healthy lifestyle. Whether you're exploring fasting, gut health, or hormonal wellness, these books, websites, and apps provide valuable insights to help you reach your goals.

Conclusion

As women navigate the complexities of health, wellness, and aging, they face unique challenges and opportunities to thrive. This book was crafted with a focus on addressing specific needs—balancing hormones, supporting gut health, managing weight, boosting energy, and reducing inflammation—all of which play central roles in a woman's journey to sustainable wellness. Through mindful practices, dietary choices, and a strategic approach to fasting, the road to a healthier life can be both achievable and empowering. In this conclusion, we will revisit the key principles shared throughout the book, examining how these practices and insights converge to support a lifestyle rooted in balance, vitality, and longevity.

Embracing the Power of Nutritional Balance

Nutrition forms the cornerstone of our well-being, impacting how we feel, think, and function each day. The recipes and meal plans in this book aim to bring harmony to a woman's body through nutrient-dense ingredients tailored to specific needs. For example, hormone-friendly ingredients like healthy fats, lean proteins, and fiber-rich foods create a foundation for lasting balance. Nutrients such as omega-3 fatty acids and vitamins D and B12 are instrumental in stabilizing hormone levels, supporting the production and regulation of key hormones.

Meal planning allows for the daily integration of these nutrients in ways that are practical and adaptable. Women often juggle multiple responsibilities—work, family, social engagements—so creating meals that are quick yet nourishing becomes essential. Each recipe in this book takes a time-conscious approach, offering meals that are easy to prepare without sacrificing nutritional quality. By following these simple recipes, women can make meal prep a manageable part of their routine, enhancing their ability to consistently support hormonal health through diet.

Balancing macronutrients and micronutrients through a variety of ingredients also helps to stave off cravings, maintain energy levels, and reduce the likelihood of mood swings. A well-rounded approach to nutrition means not just aiming for a single health benefit but targeting multiple aspects of wellness. Nutrient-dense recipes can be a strong ally in a woman's health journey, offering stability for the endocrine system, supporting optimal digestion, and keeping energy levels balanced.

Fasting for Health and Empowerment

Fasting is a concept that has seen increased interest and validation within health research, especially as it relates to women's health. Yet, it's a practice that needs to be approached with nuance and understanding, particularly for women over 40 who experience different metabolic demands. The benefits of fasting are far-reaching: it helps to manage blood sugar levels, aids in weight management, supports cellular repair, and may even extend longevity. However, fasting can impact women differently than men, making it crucial to adopt methods that respect the unique physiology of women.

The fasting strategies provided here are designed to be flexible and adaptable, giving women the freedom to experiment with different schedules while staying attuned to their bodies' responses. For example, intermittent fasting, such as the 16:8 method, allows women to harness the benefits of fasting without undue stress on their bodies. This approach gives the body time to focus on repair processes without significantly restricting energy intake. Additionally, specific meal timing around fasting breaks, focusing on nutrient-dense, gut-friendly foods, can further enhance the benefits of fasting, helping women achieve optimal energy and gut health without drastic dietary changes.

Fasting also offers a sense of empowerment. By choosing when and how to eat, women can align their eating patterns with their wellness goals, regaining control over their relationship with food. It's not about restrictive dieting or following a rigid schedule; rather, fasting enables women to make intentional, informed choices that prioritize their health and well-being. Acknowledging the flexibility of fasting schedules, this book encourages women to listen to their bodies, allowing them to tailor fasting to their needs and life circumstances. This adaptability fosters a more sustainable practice that complements the broader goals of health and longevity.

Supporting Gut Health: The Foundation of Wellness

The gut has rightly earned its title as the "second brain" because of its integral role in overall health. Gut health impacts digestion, nutrient absorption, immune function, and even mental clarity. For women, maintaining a balanced gut microbiome is essential to managing hormonal health, reducing inflammation, and achieving sustained energy levels. The recipes in this book include a variety of fiber-rich, prebiotic, and probiotic foods, all designed to nourish the gut. Ingredients like leafy greens, cruciferous vegetables, chia seeds, and fermented foods work synergistically to feed beneficial bacteria and keep the digestive tract in optimal shape.

One of the main challenges to gut health is inflammation, often stemming from processed foods, stress, and environmental toxins. Incorporating anti-inflammatory foods into the diet can mitigate these effects, helping to keep the gut lining strong and resilient. Turmeric, ginger, berries, and leafy greens are all potent anti-inflammatory agents that have been strategically included in recipes to address this issue. When gut health is prioritized, women experience clearer thinking, balanced moods, and reduced bloating, creating a solid foundation for holistic wellness.

The timing of gut-friendly foods also matters. When breaking a fast, introducing probiotic-rich foods, such as a kefir smoothie or Greek yogurt with berries, eases the digestive system into activity without overwhelming it. Prebiotic foods, such as bananas and oats, further sustain beneficial bacteria, supporting a balanced microbiome that continues to thrive long after the meal is finished. The guide on gut health and fasting practices aims to give women practical tools that reinforce their digestive health, adding layers of resilience and adaptability to their wellness routines.

Addressing Weight Management with Compassion

Weight management is a deeply personal topic for many women, and it often comes with a multitude of social and psychological pressures. This book takes a compassionate approach to weight management, emphasizing sustainable, healthy practices rather than quick fixes or restrictive diets. By integrating balanced meals, fasting, and regular intake of fiber-rich foods, women can support their metabolism in a way that respects their body's natural rhythms.

A significant focus is placed on promoting a metabolism that functions efficiently and healthily, rather than simply on calorie restriction. High-fiber foods, lean proteins, and healthy fats play key roles in maintaining satiety, stabilizing blood sugar, and supporting energy expenditure. Additionally, the anti-inflammatory ingredients woven into these recipes help reduce potential metabolic slowdowns linked to inflammation. Women over 40 often experience changes in metabolism, but through balanced eating and fasting, they can support weight management in a way that aligns with their individual health needs.

Building confidence around weight management also involves setting realistic and personalized goals. This book encourages women to focus on overall health, energy levels, and well-being rather than solely on a number on the scale. Sustainable weight management is a byproduct of consistently nourishing the body, maintaining a healthy gut, and choosing lifestyle practices that support hormone balance. By approaching weight management with kindness and patience, women can create a wellness journey that is both fulfilling and transformative.

Sustained Energy for a Vibrant Life

Energy management is a key aspect of health, especially for women juggling various roles and responsibilities. The recipes and fasting schedules in this book are designed to maintain steady energy levels, avoiding the common highs and lows associated with stimulants or refined sugars. Protein-rich breakfasts, balanced lunches, and nutrient-dense dinners ensure that energy is sustained throughout the day, supporting productivity, mood stability, and overall vitality.

Fasting naturally complements this approach by promoting metabolic flexibility, allowing the body to shift seamlessly between using glucose and fat as energy sources. When combined with meals rich in fiber, protein, and healthy fats, fasting can support steady energy release, helping women to feel focused and resilient. This approach allows women to thrive without the need for constant snacking or quick energy fixes, fostering a relationship with food that feels satisfying and balanced.

Additionally, by integrating anti-inflammatory and antioxidant-rich foods, women can enhance cellular energy production, contributing to a sustained feeling of vitality. Foods like berries, leafy greens, and fatty fish support mitochondrial health, which is essential for cellular energy production. This holistic approach to energy ensures that women can face each day with the vigor and clarity needed to embrace life's demands.

Inflammation Reduction for Long-Term Health

Chronic inflammation is a root cause of many health issues, from joint pain to skin conditions to metabolic disorders. The recipes and practices in this book focus on reducing inflammation through anti-inflammatory foods and lifestyle adjustments, fostering an environment for optimal health. Ingredients like turmeric, ginger, green tea, and fatty fish provide powerful anti-inflammatory effects, addressing inflammation at the cellular level.

Fasting plays a role in reducing inflammation as well. By giving the digestive system regular breaks, fasting can help lower oxidative stress and inflammation, allowing cells to focus on repair rather than constantly processing food. This approach supports a longer, healthier life, as inflammation is a major contributor to aging and disease progression. With the combined benefits of anti-inflammatory foods and fasting, women can feel more mobile, experience less joint pain, and enjoy healthier skin, all of which contribute to a vibrant, fulfilling life.

Looking Forward: A Holistic, Sustainable Path

The ultimate goal of this book is to empower women to embrace a lifestyle that feels sustainable, enriching, and rewarding. Every woman's health journey is unique, and there is no one-size-fits-all approach. However, by integrating mindful eating, fasting, and holistic wellness practices, women can create a framework that supports their goals and adapts to their needs. The principles and recipes shared here are designed to be flexible, allowing women to tailor them to their preferences, lifestyle, and evolving wellness goals.

In this journey toward holistic health, the aim is not perfection but consistency and self-compassion. Each small, mindful decision accumulates, contributing to an overall sense of well-being, vitality, and balance. With the information, resources, and recipes in this book, women have the tools to cultivate a lasting, harmonious relationship with their health.

Closing Thoughts

True wellness extends beyond physical health; it encompasses mental, emotional, and spiritual well-being. This book provides not only dietary guidance but also a broader perspective on wellness, supporting women in creating balanced, nourishing routines that contribute to their sense of purpose, fulfillment, and self-worth. As women navigate their unique health journeys, this holistic approach encourages them to honor their bodies, make empowered choices, and develop practices that foster resilience and vitality.

By emphasizing flexible, adaptable strategies for nutrition, fasting, and lifestyle adjustments, this book is designed to support women's wellness across various life stages and health needs. Hormone balance, gut health, energy management, weight maintenance, and inflammation reduction are interconnected aspects of well-being that evolve over time, each influencing the other. Understanding these interconnections can help women feel more in tune with their bodies, empowered by knowledge, and confident in their ability to make decisions that prioritize long-term health and joy.

This journey does not demand drastic changes or one-size-fits-all solutions. Instead, it invites women to explore their unique needs, experiment with strategies that resonate, and build sustainable habits that enhance their quality of life. Whether a woman is just beginning to explore fasting, curious about integrating more gut-friendly foods, or committed to improving her energy levels, the insights provided here serve as a starting point for positive transformation.

Health is both a personal and communal journey. As women improve their health, they often find themselves inspiring others—family, friends, colleagues, and community members—to adopt similar practices. This ripple effect creates a positive impact that extends beyond the individual, fostering a culture of health, resilience, and empowerment. In sharing these practices, recipes, and routines, women can connect with one another through shared values, mutual support, and collective knowledge.

Ultimately, this book encourages every woman to cultivate a health journey that is rooted in self-respect and self-discovery. It's about building a lifestyle that celebrates nourishment, balance, and wellness while embracing the joy of growth, adaptability, and learning. The information here is intended as a toolkit for personal empowerment, providing women with both the knowledge and confidence to live a vibrant, healthy life on their own terms.

As you move forward, remember that each step you take toward balanced eating, mindful fasting, and comprehensive wellness is a step toward becoming the healthiest, most resilient version of yourself. Celebrate the small victories, remain patient with your progress, and trust in the process of discovering what works best for you. The path to wellness is not linear, and it's okay to adapt and refine your journey along the way. What matters most is the commitment to yourself, your health, and the vibrant life that awaits you.

In honoring this commitment, you are not only supporting your physical body but also nurturing a lifestyle of empowerment and growth that will serve you for years to come. Thank you for taking this journey, for embracing wellness with open arms, and for choosing to prioritize your health, happiness, and longevity.

Bonus Chapter 1: 28-Day Meal Plan

This 28-day meal plan provides a comprehensive guide to achieving various health goals by incorporating recipes for hormone balance, gut health, sustainable weight loss, energy boosting, and anti-inflammatory support. Each week follows a balanced structure, allowing you to benefit from nutrient-dense ingredients and diverse meals while supporting overall wellness. Meals are strategically selected to maximize results by aligning with the specific health benefits discussed in this book.

Day	Breakfast	Lunch	Dinner
1	1. Hormone-Balancing Avocado & Berry Smoothie	13. Kale & Sweet Potato Hormone Salad	25. Wild-Caught Salmon with Roasted Asparagus
2	2. Chia & Flaxseed Power Oatmeal	15. Lentil & Avocado Buddha Bowl	30. Hormone-Supporting Mushroom & Spinach Stir Fry
3	3. Apple & Cinnamon Quinoa Porridge	16. Roasted Beet & Walnut Salad	29. Grilled Cod with Brussels Sprouts & Carrots
4	5. Almond & Seed Breakfast Bowl	17. Mediterranean Chickpea & Feta Salad	31. Ginger Chicken with Roasted Vegetables
5	6. Green Tea & Almond Smoothie	20. Citrus Chicken & Spinach Salad	34. Quinoa Stuffed Bell Peppers
6	7. Berry & Protein Yogurt Parfait	21. Roasted Squash & Spinach Salad	35. Spicy Lentil & Veggie Curry
7	8. Golden Milk Overnight Oats	19. Collard Green Wraps with Tofu & Mixed Greens	36. Herb-Marinated Grilled Tofu
8	109. Probiotic Greek Yogurt & Berries Bowl	121. Kimchi & Cabbage Salad with Sesame Dressing	133. Baked Miso Cod with Bok Choy
9	110. Prebiotic Oats with Chia Seeds	123. Collard Wraps with Avocado & Pickles	136. Sauerkraut & Herb Salad with Grilled Fish
10	111. Fermented Sauerkraut & Veggie Scramble	122. Gut-Healthy Miso Soup with Tofu	137. Turmeric-Spiced Lentil Soup
11	112. Kefir Smoothie with Banana	124. Lentil Salad with Gut-Boosting Dressing	138. Gut-Healing Roasted Squash & Broccoli

12	113. Chia Pudding with Blueberries	128. Mixed Greens with Avocado & Fermented Veggies	139. Fermented Kimchi Veggie Stir Fry
13	114. Gut-Friendly Oatmeal with Seeds	129. Probiotic Chicken Salad with Yogurt	140. Miso-Glazed Salmon with Greens
14	115. Ginger & Apple Smoothie	130. Sautéed Mushrooms & Greens Salad	134. Roasted Garlic & Veggie Broth Soup
15	74. Low-Calorie Berry & Almond Smoothie	50. Quinoa & Black Bean Salad	62. Zucchini Noodles with Basil Pesto Chicken
16	75. High-Protein Greek Yogurt & Chia Bowl	52. Sweet Potato & Black Bean Tacos	63. Lentil & Veggie Soup with Fresh Herbs
17	76. Avocado & Smoked Salmon Plate	54. Greek-Inspired Turkey Salad with Olives	28. Black Bean & Sweet Potato Enchiladas
18	77. Cinnamon-Spiced Overnight Oats	59. Grilled Veggie & Hummus Wrap	65. Stuffed Bell Peppers with Ground Turkey
19	78. Low-Carb Cauliflower & Cheese Frittata	58. Salmon & Avocado Energy Bowl	102. Roasted Brussels Sprouts with Chicken Sausage
20	79. Spinach & Feta Egg Muffins	93. Chickpea & Spinach Protein Salad	71. Quinoa & Veggie Stuffed Zucchini Boats
21	80. Keto-Friendly Nut Butter Smoothie	56. Edamame & Mixed Greens Bowl	29. Grilled Cod with Brussels Sprouts & Carrots
22	37. Almond Butter & Banana Smoothie	14. Spinach Wrap with Hummus & Sprouts	64. Garlic Shrimp with Cauliflower Rice
23	38. Veggie & Egg Scramble with Avocado	57. Roasted Chickpea Salad with Tahini Dressing	33. Basil Pesto Zoodles with Shrimp
24	39. Oatmeal with Hemp Seeds & Fresh Fruit	20. Citrus Chicken & Spinach Salad	107. Grilled Veggie Kebabs with Lean Beef
25	40. Matcha Green Tea Smoothie	94. Zucchini Noodle Bowl with Fresh Basil	108. Light Stuffed Portobello Mushrooms
26	41. Protein-Packed Cottage Cheese & Berry Bowl	128. Mixed Greens with Avocado & Fermented Veggies	155. Anti-Inflammatory Stuffed Bell Peppers with Rice

| 27 | 42. Peanut Butter & Chia Toast | 149. Sweet Potato & Kale Salad | 154. Sautéed Greens with Roasted Sweet Potatoes |
| 28 | 44. High-Protein Greek Yogurt Parfait | 129. Probiotic Chicken Salad with Yogurt | 102. Roasted Brussels Sprouts with Chicken Sausage |

Bonus Chapter 2: Special Tips Inspired by Dr. Mindy Pelz's Teachings

Dr. Mindy Pelz has dedicated her work to helping women harness the power of fasting, hormone balance, and holistic wellness practices, particularly for those navigating hormonal changes in their 40s and beyond. This bonus chapter provides some of her most valuable insights on aligning diet, fasting, and lifestyle practices with women's health needs. These tips are designed to guide women in creating sustainable routines that support their unique hormonal cycles, improve energy, enhance metabolic health, and foster longevity.

Tip 1: Sync Your Fasting with Your Menstrual Cycle

One of Dr. Pelz's primary teachings is the importance of syncing fasting schedules with the menstrual cycle for optimal hormonal balance. Fasting affects hormones like cortisol, estrogen, and progesterone, which fluctuate throughout the month. By adjusting fasting schedules to align with these hormonal changes, women can experience a smoother, more balanced fasting journey without the hormonal disruptions that can sometimes accompany prolonged fasting.

➢ **Days 1-10 (Menstruation to Early Follicular Phase)**: This is an ideal time to ease into fasting, especially with shorter fasts like the 13-15 hour range. Hormones are relatively low, making it a good time to experiment with fasting for cellular repair without over-stressing the body.
➢ **Days 11-16 (Ovulation)**: During ovulation, estrogen and testosterone levels rise, leading to increased energy and metabolic benefits. This is a great time to try a longer fast, such as a 16:8 schedule, to maximize energy use and potential fat-burning benefits.
➢ **Days 17-28 (Luteal Phase)**: The luteal phase, leading up to menstruation, is marked by an increase in progesterone, which creates a need for more stability and nourishment. Dr. Pelz recommends reducing fasting hours or even avoiding fasting altogether during this phase to support progesterone production. Instead, focus on nutrient-dense meals rich in healthy fats, fiber, and carbohydrates, such as sweet potatoes, nuts, and leafy greens.

By aligning fasting with hormonal fluctuations, women can optimize the benefits of fasting without disrupting their natural cycles or experiencing negative side effects.

Tip 2: Break Your Fast with "Hormone-Feeding" Foods

When breaking a fast, the first foods you eat matter greatly. Dr. Pelz emphasizes the importance of choosing nutrient-dense, hormone-supportive foods that nourish and sustain energy levels. Foods rich in healthy fats, fiber, and proteins are particularly beneficial, as they support stable blood sugar levels, promote satiety, and minimize cortisol spikes.

➢ **Avocado**: Packed with monounsaturated fats, avocado supports hormone production and helps stabilize blood sugar after fasting.

➢ **Eggs**: A versatile source of protein, eggs are nutrient-dense and help stabilize blood sugar levels, making them a perfect choice to end a fast.

➢ **Leafy Greens**: Rich in fiber, antioxidants, and essential vitamins, greens like spinach and kale support liver health, which is essential for hormone metabolism.

Dr. Pelz suggests breaking fasts with a combination of these foods to support a stable and nourishing transition into your eating window. A smoothie with avocado, spinach, and a scoop of plant-based protein, or an egg scramble with vegetables, are great examples of hormone-feeding meals to break your fast.

Tip 3: Practice "Fasting Variability" to Adapt to Your Body's Needs

"Fasting variability" is a concept Dr. Pelz often advocates for, encouraging women to be flexible and adaptive with their fasting schedules. Instead of adhering strictly to the same fasting schedule daily, fasting variability involves adjusting fasting lengths based on how the body feels, energy levels, and life demands. This approach helps women avoid overstressing their systems, especially if they are balancing work, family, and other commitments.

For example, during stressful periods, women might shorten their fasting windows, practicing 12-13 hour fasts instead of longer fasts. On calmer days, they might experiment with 16-hour fasts. The goal is to create a fasting routine that feels sustainable and responsive to changing life circumstances. Fasting variability allows for better mental and physical adaptation, enabling women to harness the benefits of fasting without creating undue strain.

Tip 4: Incorporate "Feasting Days" to Support Metabolism

Dr. Pelz emphasizes the importance of "feasting days" as a way to support metabolic health and prevent the body from adapting too much to caloric restriction. On a feasting day, women are encouraged to eat more freely, prioritizing whole, nutrient-dense foods without the constraints of a fasting window. Feasting days help to "re-feed" the body, support hormone production, and provide the body with a metabolic reset.

Typically, Dr. Pelz recommends having one to two feasting days per week. This approach allows the body to stay flexible, prevent metabolic slowdowns, and sustain energy without the feeling of deprivation. Ideal feasting day meals include a balance of proteins, healthy fats, and complex carbohydrates, such as grilled salmon with quinoa and roasted vegetables, or a breakfast of Greek yogurt with berries and chia seeds.

Tip 5: Prioritize Gut Health to Enhance Fasting Benefits

Gut health is a foundational element of overall wellness, and Dr. Pelz frequently highlights its importance in a fasting regimen. A healthy gut can improve digestion, support hormone regulation, and reduce inflammation, all of which contribute to a more effective fasting experience. Dr. Pelz recommends incorporating prebiotic and probiotic foods to support gut health and enhance the benefits of fasting.

> **Prebiotic Foods**: Foods like garlic, onions, asparagus, and bananas feed beneficial gut bacteria, promoting a balanced microbiome that can better support the body during fasting.

> **Probiotic Foods**: Yogurt, kefir, kimchi, and sauerkraut introduce beneficial bacteria into the gut, aiding in digestion and supporting immune health.

Breaking a fast with gut-supportive foods such as a kefir smoothie or a yogurt bowl with berries can create a smooth, gentle transition for the digestive system. Incorporating these foods throughout your meals also helps maintain digestive health, allowing for better nutrient absorption and sustained energy.

Tip 6: Use Time-Restricted Eating to Boost Energy and Productivity

Time-restricted eating is a fasting approach that narrows the eating window each day, allowing the body to rest and reset for a longer period. Dr. Pelz often emphasizes that narrowing the eating window to eight or even six hours can lead to improved energy and productivity, as it allows the body to spend more time in a "fasted" state where it can focus on repair and cellular rejuvenation.

Women who are new to time-restricted eating can start with a 12-hour eating window and gradually work their way to an 8-hour window. During the eating window, it's essential to prioritize nutrient-dense foods and avoid refined sugars and processed snacks, which can cause energy crashes. With time-restricted eating, women often find they have more sustained energy, fewer cravings, and an enhanced focus throughout the day.

Tip 7: Listen to Your Body and Adjust Accordingly

Dr. Pelz's most important advice centers around the concept of listening to your body. She believes that fasting, like any health practice, should feel empowering and supportive rather than restrictive. Women are encouraged to stay attuned to their body's signals—whether they're experiencing fatigue, hunger, or stress—and to adjust fasting schedules or dietary choices accordingly.

For instance, if fasting starts to feel draining or creates anxiety, it may be a sign to shorten fasting windows or introduce more feasting days. Similarly, if energy levels are high, experimenting with a slightly longer fast could provide an additional boost. Flexibility and mindfulness are key, allowing fasting and dietary practices to work with the body's natural rhythms rather than against them.

Closing Thoughts on Dr. Pelz's Approach

The teachings of Dr. Mindy Pelz offer a blueprint for women to take control of their health in a way that feels adaptable, science-based, and in harmony with their unique needs. By syncing fasting with the menstrual cycle, prioritizing hormone-feeding foods, and embracing fasting variability and feasting days, women can craft a wellness routine that is not only effective but also sustainable. Dr. Pelz's approach promotes balance, encouraging women to listen to their bodies, prioritize nutrient-dense meals, and view fasting as a flexible tool rather than a rigid protocol.

Whether you are new to fasting or well-versed in its benefits, the insights in this chapter offer valuable strategies to personalize your wellness journey. Remember, the path to health is not about perfection; it's about creating habits that support you, empower you, and bring balance to your daily life.

Bonus Chapter 3: A Comprehensive Guide to Fasting

Fasting has become a powerful practice in wellness, blending both ancient traditions and modern science. It's a method that allows the body to reset, repair, and improve overall health, focusing on "when" rather than "what" we eat. Through this chapter, we'll explore fasting's benefits, different types, and practical ways to incorporate it into daily life, especially for women over 40 who experience unique hormonal and metabolic shifts.

Fasting is essentially a voluntary pause in food consumption for a set period, shifting the body from reliance on glucose to stored fat as an energy source. When eating ceases, insulin levels drop, prompting the body to begin using fat for fuel. This change activates several metabolic processes, including fat burning and cellular repair, offering potential improvements in metabolic health, weight balance, and longevity. Fasting's appeal also lies in its flexibility; it doesn't require a rigid diet plan but allows you to choose when to eat, making it a sustainable addition to various lifestyles.

The body responds well to fasting in several ways. First, by shifting to stored fat for fuel, the body becomes more metabolically flexible, which can support weight balance and improve blood sugar control. Additionally, fasting can trigger a process called autophagy, where cells remove damaged components, essentially "cleaning out" cellular waste, aiding in rejuvenation and potentially slowing aging. Fasting also plays a role in hormone regulation, especially insulin and cortisol. For women, balancing these hormones can have profound effects on energy levels and overall well-being. There's also evidence that fasting increases mental clarity by enhancing the body's production of ketones, which provide steady energy to the brain.

Gut health is another area where fasting shows promise. By giving the digestive system periodic rest, fasting may help lower gut inflammation, encourage a balanced microbiome, and support nutrient absorption. Fasting's emphasis on meal timing over food types also helps women develop healthier, more mindful relationships with food, contributing to emotional and mental well-being.

Fasting comes in various forms, allowing women to select an approach that fits their lifestyle and health goals. Intermittent fasting, one of the most accessible types, involves alternating between eating and fasting within a 24-hour period. The 16:8 method, where you fast for 16 hours and eat within an 8-hour window, is popular for beginners because it allows for adequate fasting without extreme restriction. Another version is the 14:10 method, with a 14-hour fasting period and a 10-hour eating window, which is more flexible and can be a good starting point for those new to fasting.

Alternate day fasting involves fasting every other day, either abstaining from food entirely or limiting intake to about 500 calories. This approach allows for deeper cellular repair, though it can be demanding and is better suited for those who have some fasting experience. The 5:2 diet is another method where you eat normally five days a week and restrict calorie intake on two non-consecutive days. This approach offers the benefits of fasting without the daily commitment. Extended fasting, often lasting 24 hours or longer, is more intensive and best suited for those well-versed in fasting.

For those new to fasting, starting gradually can make the transition smoother. Begin with a 12-hour fast, such as from 8 pm to 8 am, to get accustomed to the rhythm. Gradually extend this fasting period to 14 or 16 hours over time, allowing your body to adjust to longer periods without food. Staying hydrated during fasting is essential, as it prevents dehydration and helps manage hunger. Water, herbal teas, or black coffee (without cream or sugar) are excellent choices. Listening to your body throughout the process is key; if you experience extreme fatigue, lightheadedness, or other discomforts, it may be best to shorten the fast.

When breaking a fast, nutrient-dense, easy-to-digest foods are ideal. Choose options rich in healthy fats, proteins, and fiber to provide lasting energy and avoid blood sugar spikes. For instance, starting with a smoothie containing avocado, spinach, and a protein source offers a gentle, balanced way to nourish the body post-fast. Other great options include eggs, leafy greens, and yogurt, all of which support sustained energy and gut health.

A successful fasting experience benefits from a mindful approach, one that considers the purpose behind the fast. Setting clear, realistic goals, such as enhancing mental clarity, supporting metabolic health, or simply exploring new dietary practices, can help maintain motivation. Trying different fasting schedules is often necessary to find what best aligns with your needs. Some may thrive on a daily 16:8 schedule, while others might benefit more from occasional extended fasts or the 5:2 diet. Fasting's flexibility allows for experimentation, so it's okay to adjust your routine as you learn more about how fasting impacts your energy, mood, and health.

Focusing on nutrient-dense foods during eating windows supports health goals without the need for strict dieting. By prioritizing whole foods, you create balanced meals that provide the necessary vitamins, minerals, and antioxidants, aiding in recovery and reducing cravings during fasting periods. Integrating mindfulness into fasting periods enhances the experience; fasting can serve as an opportunity for mental clarity and reflection. Simple practices like meditation, light movement, or journaling complement the physical rest that fasting provides, creating a more holistic wellness routine.

Though fasting offers significant benefits, it can also come with challenges, particularly for those new to the practice. Some people may experience fatigue, cravings, or even irritability in the beginning. Hunger during the early stages of fasting is common, but as the body adapts, many find that these symptoms lessen or disappear. Consistency, patience, and a gradual approach are essential to navigating these initial hurdles.

For women, fasting requires a specific approach due to the unique effects of hormonal fluctuations. Many women benefit from adjusting fasting schedules to align with their menstrual cycle, as fasting impacts hormones like cortisol, estrogen, and progesterone. During menstruation and the early follicular phase, women are often more resilient to fasting and can incorporate longer fasts, such as the 16:8 method. However, in the luteal phase (days 17-28), when the body needs more energy to support higher progesterone levels, women may benefit from shorter fasts or even reducing fasting frequency.

Finally, fasting encourages a deep, reflective connection to food, hunger, and satiety. This practice can offer insight into emotional eating habits and allow for a more conscious, satisfying relationship with nourishment. Instead of seeing fasting as a form of restriction, many find it to be a way of resetting both body and mind, creating space to focus on other aspects of life beyond food. For those seeking more than just physical benefits, fasting can be a transformative experience, fostering resilience, self-discipline, and an appreciation for one's natural rhythms and needs.

In conclusion, fasting is a versatile and powerful tool for supporting overall health. By understanding its science, types, and approaches, you can create a fasting practice that's tailored to your body's needs, your lifestyle, and your wellness goals.

Made in the USA
Las Vegas, NV
03 January 2025

15774675R00070